Development for Academic Leaders

A Practical Guide for Fundraising Success

Penelepe C. Hunt

Foreword by John Lippincott

JOSSEY-BASS
A Wiley Imprint
www.josseybass.com

Published by Jossey-Bass
A Wiley Imprint
One Montgomery Street, Suite 1200
San Francisco, CA 94104-4594—www.josseybass.com

Library of Congress Cataloging-in-Publication Data
Hunt, Penelepe C., date. author.
  Development for academic leaders : a practical guide for fundraising success / Penelepe C. Hunt. – First edition.
        pages cm. – (The Jossey-Bass Higher and Adult Education Series)
  Includes bibliographical references and index.
  ISBN 978-1-118-27017-2 (hardback); ISBN 978-1-118-28631-9 (ebk);
ISBN 978-1-118-28350-9 (ebk); ISBN 978-1-118-28487-2 (ebk)
  1. Educational fund raising–United States. I. Title.
  LB2336.H86 2012
  379.1'3–dc23

Printed in the United States of America
FIRST EDITION
HB Printing   10 9 8 7 6 5 4 3

The Jossey-Bass Higher and Adult Education Series

Contents

For Jaye, my Precious daughter

Foreword

Fundraising has become an essential element in the job descriptions of department heads, deans, and provosts at colleges and universities in North America and increasingly around the world. This important responsibility has been added to the already complex role of these academic leaders both because they are strategic partners in the fundraising process and because fundraising is a strategic component of academic planning.

Indeed, the academic leadership is often in the best position to inspire potential donors by clearly and passionately articulating the vision for a given program or project and the impact it will have on students and society.

Having responsibility for a role, however, doesn't always mean one is comfortable with it. In fact, academic leaders (including presidents) frequently report that fundraising is the responsibility for which they feel the least prepared. Precisely because they are experts in their disciplines and have distinguished themselves in their departments, they have had little opportunity to gain experience in fundraising or any of the other areas of institutional advancement. Academic leaders have little choice but to embrace their role in fundraising, yet many are reluctant to do so out of concern that it will compromise their integrity, out of discomfort with the act of asking for money, out of fear of rejection, or simply out of unfamiliarity with the process.

Fundraising is, in fact, a noble activity that can be enormously gratifying and endlessly interesting. After all, it is not so much about the money as it is about aligning a donor's passion with an institution's vision. It's about providing resources to help students improve their lives and researchers improve our world. Fundraising combines the art of human relationships with sound business practices, including strategic research, planning, and communication.

Fundraising is also about partnerships. Academic leaders need to forge productive partnerships not only with current and prospective donors but also with the institution's professional fundraising staff. Whether those staff work within the academic department or within a central office, they are an essential resource and a key ally in building and sustaining an effective fundraising program.

Among professional fundraisers, one of the most knowledgeable and certainly one of the most successful at partnering with academic leaders is Penny Hunt.

Penny has overseen successful fundraising programs at public and private institutions, including the University of Illinois at Chicago, where she instituted a monthly dean's training program; Northwestern University, where she directed a successful $1.5 billion comprehensive campaign; and Pomona College, where she managed the annual fund.

She has also served as a management consultant and executive coach for numerous academic leaders, helping them not only to understand the fundraising process but to find real joy in it. She has consistently earned top ratings as a presenter at the "Development for Deans" and "Advanced Development for Deans" conferences offered by the Council for Advancement and Support of Education (CASE). And she is frequently called upon to provide "CASE on Campus" workshops that bring together all of the academic leaders at an institution for specialized training.

In short, when it comes to fundraising for academic leaders, Penny wrote the book . . . literally. In the pages that follow, she demystifies the art of fundraising, provides practical and down-to-earth guidance, and bridges the gap between academic leaders and fundraising professionals. She addresses the concerns, the discomfort, the fears, and the unfamiliarity that stand as barriers to success. Most important, she offers the insights and the inspiration that academic leaders need to approach fundraising with confidence and enthusiasm.

This book, then, is an essential read for both current and aspiring academic leaders, an important addition to the body of knowledge in educational fundraising, and a significant contribution to the advancement of higher education.

John Lippincott
President
Council for Advancement and Support of Education

Part One

Development and Academic Leaders

1

The Role of Academic Leaders in Development

Development has become a part of every academic leader's job. Scan the ads in the *Chronicle of Higher Education*, and you will find that nearly every one for a dean, president, or provost includes a reference to fundraising as part of the position.

Rare is the university that can give its colleges everything they need, or want, in order to be the best they can be. Academics and program heads who passively rely on traditional sources of funding will be left behind by other programs in their own university and by peer colleges in other universities. To excel in garnering new resources, academic leaders must be creative, entrepreneurial, and proactive.

Securing private support is primarily the responsibility of the development office, whether the central campus program or a development staff within your program. Many of the gifts your college receives will result from the direct work of these staff. Academic heads who rely solely on the development staff can count on receiving small current use gifts and the occasional larger outright gift or bequest.

Those who become personally involved in development can expect much more. A donor who is considering making a major investment in your program will almost always want to know you, understand your vision, assess your leadership, and feel confident that you can steward the gift wisely. Development officers can explain your college or program and the work you do. But no one can say it in quite the same way as you can. It is your field, your leadership, your vision, and your faculty, and donors want to hear all of that personally from you.

Some academics love development and are highly effective at it. It comes naturally to them, and they happily make it a high priority. Others tolerate it, engaging somewhat hesitantly and reluctantly. Still others avoid it at all costs. Not surprisingly, those in the first category are the most successful and raise the most money. Donors can tell when an academic is genuinely enjoying development work, and they respond accordingly.

If you are in the second category, do not despair. Many academics begin their engagement with development expecting not to like it. Over time, many find it to be one of the most enjoyable parts of their job.

The most common concern new academic leaders express about development is that it will be like sales. They imagine they will be trying to extract money from people who do not want to give it up. Nothing could be further from the truth. When donors talk about giving, they usually mention feeling joyful, happy, and fulfilled. As you will see in subsequent chapters, giving comes from a partnership that forms between you and the donor, where you both share the ultimate goal of advancing your program. Once you experience that process, you will begin to see why some academics love it. And in fact, you might become one of those enthusiastic fundraisers.

Academics who love fundraising and excel at it are fondly called *development deans*, *development presidents*, or the equivalent title by their development colleagues. What makes those academics so good at development is not the ability to "sell." It is the commitment in spirit and in time they make to the work. They are available for development purposes and are genuinely committed to development work. They do not just go through the motions. Development academics have a vision and a plan for their programs and can articulate it in person and in writing. They love their programs, and their vision for what their programs can become is contagious. They enjoy their internal and external constituencies. This is more than a job for a development academic; it is a passion.

Universities appoint academics to leadership positions based on their academic and administrative achievements and then expect them to be seasoned major gift officers their first day on the job. The majority of academics who are not successful at development simply lack a solid knowledge base for how to be effective in an area that is new to them. This book introduces you to the concepts and practices you need in order to be a successful fundraising leader.

Public Universities and Private Philanthropy

Public universities entered the world of fundraising decades later than private universities. And many academics who are entering the world of development have spent their careers in public universities. Therefore, academics who have advanced their careers in public universities may not have had significant exposure to fundraising programs as they have advanced through the faculty ranks.

Traditionally public universities had a reliable source of income from their state legislatures; private philanthropy was not part of the picture. By the early 1980s, the major public universities began to recognize that basic funding from their states would provide them only with the resources necessary to be good universities. To be great, they needed more, and so they began to pursue private philanthropy for that margin of excellence beyond the baseline state funding and the federal research dollars their faculty were securing. Through the 1990s and the early 2000s, more and more state universities began exploring private philanthropy. As state resources allocated to universities began to decline, the universities' reasons for pursuing private philanthropy expanded from merely seeking the icing on the cake to realizing they needed private support to provide the basic ingredients for the cake itself.

Public universities newly entering the development world are at a disadvantage for several reasons:

- Their alumni were not trained from their first years in college to think of the university as needing their philanthropic support. Many private colleges and universities start this training from the moment the students are admitted.

- The public, including alumni, often do not realize that the university is no longer fully supported by the state.

- Some state legislatures view funds raised from private sources as a replacement for public allocations.

Academics in these universities can especially benefit from engaging in development. It is a buffer against growing budget cuts as state support declines.

Development Versus Advancement

As you enter the world of fundraising, you will commonly hear the terms *development* and *advancement*. They are frequently used interchangeably, but are fundamentally different.

Development refers to fundraising and all the steps involved in the process of raising money.

Advancement is a broader term that encompasses all of the functions related to advancing the cause of a program or university externally. The traditional advancement model is a partnership among development, alumni relations, and communications. Many programs now expand on that model to include admissions, government relations, community relations, public relations, and other functions responsible for relationships with external constituencies.

This book is primarily a guide for your work in development, though I occasionally expand the focus to encompass other areas of advancement.

An Academic's Role

Your development staff, explored in depth in the next chapter, will do the vast majority of the work of the development program. Given the many demands on your time, you should use what time you have available for strategic development, engaging in activities that only you can do.

Your primary roles in the development process are to inspire potential donors, assist donors in investing in your program, and ensure that donors' gifts are properly managed and implemented. These roles involve a variety of activities, ranging from interacting with high-end prospective donors to lending your voice to the themes and messages of the annual fund. In all of your development work, you are the face of your program, the person to whom donors entrust their contributions.

We begin by looking at your relationship with the development staff.

2

Staffing

As the head of your unit's program, you cannot balance all of your other responsibilities and run the development office too. A strong development staff will ensure that the portion of your time devoted to development is well spent. They will also ensure that the many components of a successful development program are implemented properly without the need for your direct involvement.

University-Level Staffing Models

The staffing structure of development programs at large universities ranges across a spectrum from highly centralized to highly decentralized. The nature of your own development staffing will be determined by your university's overall development staffing structure.

Highly Centralized

The chief development officer for the campus is both budgetarily and managerially responsible for all development staff. The officer's salary is paid from a central budget, and the reporting lines are solid to central development managers. While it is common in this structure to have development officers assigned to colleges and major programs, the heads of these units generally do not have any managerial authority over the officers. Program heads may or may not be involved in the hiring and assignment process for their assigned development officer. Fundraising priorities are determined centrally, and prospect management is tightly controlled by the central office. (For more on prospect management, see Chapter Four.)

Highly Decentralized

The fundraising strength in this model is heavily weighted toward colleges and major programs. Unit heads pay for and hire their own development staff, and the officers have a solid-line managerial report within the program. The central development office is small. There may be some major gift officers in the central office, but the central managers have no authority over program-based officers. The majority of the central office staffing is in development programs that are most efficiently implemented across the campus. These may include gift processing and accounting, special events, annual giving implementation (primarily direct mail and phonathons), and database management. Prospect management assignments may be documented centrally, but there is little or no central coordination of prospect assignments.

Central-Decentral Blend

Responsibility for and management of development programs and staff are shared between the central development office managers and heads of colleges and programs. The central office provides staffing for shared programs, as in the highly decentralized model. Funding for salaries and programs flows from both the central budget and unit budgets. Unit-based staff have a shared reporting line to their assigned program and to central development, though the nature of that line varies. It can be solid to both, solid to central and dotted to the unit, or solid to the unit and dotted to central. Whatever the nature of the reporting lines, unit heads and central managers collaborate on hiring decisions, performance expectations and evaluations, and compensation decisions.

Before You Begin Staffing

When determining your own staffing setup, begin by identifying and understanding the model your university uses. An in-depth conversation with the university's chief development officer can clarify the parameters within which you will be staffing your development efforts.

Your Team

Your development staff size and structure should be calibrated to your program's performance and capacity. Baseline staffing for a new program should be a single development officer, full or half time, and at least half of a support position. In a highly centralized model, you may be assigned this first officer, and you may have to begin by sharing an officer with another unit.

This initial officer should focus on building capacity wherever your program can find it. Generally this begins with an annual giving program, from which the development officer will begin to cultivate major gift prospects (more on this process in Chapters Seven and Fourteen). The development officer will also try to identify major gift prospects through a variety of other means. It takes time for donor relationships to evolve to a major gift level. You may need as long as two years to begin to see financial benefits from this initial staffing investment.

While it would be ideal to have this initial officer working solely on generating philanthropic income, this may not be possible in the early days of a development program. The officer will need to spend time building basic program infrastructure to properly implement annual giving vehicles and manage the flow of data and gifts. If you do not have staffing in other advancement areas, primarily alumni relations and communications, your development officer may have to spend time on these programs as well.

Fundraising does not succeed in a vacuum, and your constituency will be more forthcoming with gifts if they are also engaged through alumni programs and regular communication.

As the program grows, you will come to a time when your single officer is working at or above full capacity. He or she will have a very full load of program responsibilities and active donor relationships. This is a time to evaluate whether the program has also reached full capacity in terms of fundraising potential. If you and your development team, including your colleagues in the central development office, can identify reasonable growth targets that could be met with additional effort and additional potential donors with whom relationships could be developed, investing in additional staff resources is reasonable. This may entail increasing your main development officer assignment from part time to full time or, if you already have a full-time officer, expanding your staff.

Your next investment should facilitate your main development officer's having more time to spend on your highest-return program, typically work with individual donors. Hiring a second officer to specialize in annual giving or in other advancement areas such as alumni relations and communications removes those time-consuming programmatic responsibilities. This frees your main development officer to spend additional time building donor relationships and moving those relationships toward solicitation of large gifts.

As your program continues to mature, you will once again reach a point where your staff are working at capacity. This is another occasion to assess the program's performance and potential to determine whether additional investment would produce additional results. A common next step in staff expansion is to have an additional major gift officer working with individual donors or a staff member focused on foundation and corporate giving.

With each additional investment comes a new growth period before the investment provides full returns. Comprehensive and clear tracking of program performance will help you and your development colleagues assess when and how these investments are bearing fruit.

In every case, it is important to expand support staff incrementally as you expand development staff. In these days of lean budgets, scarce resources, and personally accessible technology, most academic leaders carry a larger load of their own administrative support work than they would have in the past. This is true for development officers as well. However, there are numerous components of administrative work within a development program in addition to the officer's personal clerical or secretarial tasks. Data entry and management of the database, gift processing and receipting, prospect research, and the extensive documentation associated with donor contacts are critical tasks; they are also time-consuming. Any time that development officers spend on these tasks is time not spent raising money. In addition, the skills and talents that make an officer good at negotiating large gifts may not make that same officer good at the detailed work of data maintenance and gift documentation. A modest investment in clerical support will pay significant dividends in development officer productivity and in the thorough and accurate underpinnings of the program.

Hiring

The nature of your university's overall development structure will determine who has hiring authority for your assigned development officer. But even if the central development office has complete authority in this area, you should participate in all hiring and staffing decisions. Your relationship with your development officer is critical to the success of your program. A wise development manager would never pair a development officer with an academic without first ensuring that the academic was not just comfortable with the choice but enthusiastic about it.

The same is true for you with the central development office if you are the primary hiring authority. Engaging central development in the process of selecting your development officer gives you access to development managerial expertise in areas such as performance expectations and metrics, training, and professional development. For your program to be effective, your development staff must be as much a part of the campus's development community as they are part of your college's community. Collaborating with the central development office in recruiting and hiring your development officer sets the stage for that dual citizenship from the beginning of the relationship.

Good development officers are highly skilled professionals, yet there is no single channel in which they are trained and educated. CFRE International offers an excellent certification program, the Certified Fundraising Executive. However, it is a voluntary program, and only a small fraction of fundraisers pursue it. Without an established set of credentials to review, you must evaluate candidates on a range of objective and subjective criteria.

A lead development officer for your program should have several years of direct fundraising experience that matches your program's current capacity and reasonable plans for its growth. If you have a nascent program, you can benefit from a chief development officer with a few years of annual giving or low-level major gifts experience. If your program is large and robust, you need more years of experience, working with much larger programs and higher-level donors. Building a program and running an established program require different skill sets. Be sure that your candidates have experience in the category that matches your program's stage of maturity.

It is not necessary for a candidate's experience to be in programs exactly like your own. The size of the program and the nature of the candidate's responsibilities within it are more important than the specific subject matter of his or her past organizations. If you are in a large university, experience with complex organizational structures will be a plus for your development officer, though this is a component of the culture that can be learned if it has not already been experienced.

Good development officers have impeccable integrity and are excellent listeners. The best candidates will have sophisticated questions for everyone they meet during the process, will listen carefully to the answers, and will show that they have synthesized the information as the search process moves along. Good development officers have a passion for the programs that employ them. Although they need not be subject matter experts in your area, they need to care about it, believe in it, and have an enthusiasm for it that will be contagious to potential supporters. The best officers are goal oriented. They will want to know what their performance expectations would be and how their performance would be evaluated.

The most important relationship this development officer will have is with you. If you do not feel a comfortable chemistry with a candidate from the beginning, it is likely that there is a better match for you in another candidate. The chemistry with other development officers and managers is important as well, and you should take their feedback on the candidates seriously.

Involve a wide range of your college community in the interview process, even though the ultimate decision is yours and your central development partner's. The input you get from others will give you a sense of how this candidate would fit into your program culture. These meetings give the candidate an opportunity to assess his or her future colleagues and partners and whether this culture would be a good fit from that perspective.

Relationship and Roles

A healthy partnership between an academic leader and a development staff member begins with mutual trust and mutual respect. You and your development officer must be completely in sync, and this may be your closest working relationship. Your efforts should be coordinated and based on mutually agreed-on goals. You must have crystal-clear communication with your development officer. The two of you must present a seamless, unified front about development within your program and about your program to potential donors.

To ensure that your development time is used most effectively, we—that is, your development colleagues—seek a division of responsibilities rather than a duplication of responsibilities. To achieve this:

o *You articulate your program vision.* The development officer articulates development program strategies. Development should never set program priorities. Our role is to advise you about the likelihood of securing private support for these programs and to work hard to secure that support. The vision itself must come from the unit head and the faculty. Similarly, unless you have significant experience in development, your development officer will have a better understanding of how to structure the program and deploy staff and other resources.

o *You define financial priorities.* The development officer matches prospects to opportunities. Remember that donors will do what they want to do with their money. Development officers, no matter how good they are, cannot force donors to support areas they are not interested in. Listen to your development officer's assessment of the likelihood of donor support for a project, and set your financial plans accordingly.

o *You serve as the ultimate authority figure for your program.* The development officer serves as your representative and advance person. Your development officer represents you in the donor community, preparing the way for you to enter into relationships with potential donors.

o *You set an example for faculty and staff.* The development officer finds meaningful opportunities for faculty and staff to participate. Your program community takes its cues from you. If you enjoy development and share your experiences with them, they will be more comfortable engaging in the process. As we will explore in

Chapter Twenty-One, there are important roles for faculty, staff, and students to play in a successful development program. You set the tone, and your development staff members then find the best way for members of your community to participate.

○ *You run your program.* The development officer runs the development office. The best partnerships respect this, and neither party attempts to do the other's job.

What You Should Expect from Your Development Staff

Staff should be responsive to your priorities. They should tell you if a project is not likely to secure significant donor support. And then they should work aggressively to find support for your top priorities.

They should feed the beast. And by "beast," I do not mean you. I mean the process. It takes a lot of work to establish relationships with potential donors and develop those relationships to the point where you should be involved. Development is a numbers game. We must always be expanding the pool of potential donors. One of the most important roles of the development staff is making these initial contacts. Once contact is established, the officers work with the potential donor to build a relationship and attempt to secure a gift. Some of these potential donors will be likely to give at a level where your personal involvement is justified.

Not all attempted contacts are successful. We may not have current contact information, the potential donor may not respond to our attempts to make contact, or the person may overtly decline to connect. In new programs, where there has not been a lot of general contact with alumni, it can be very difficult to make these connections.

Here are some representative figures:

- For every four phone numbers dialed, one contact is made.

- For every three contacts made, one person agrees to a face-to-face visit.

- Of every three first visits, one person eventually becomes a major donor.

- Of every three major donors, one needs your direct involvement.

Working these numbers in reverse, you can see that for every one person this development officer recommends that you work with, the officer has secured three donors, had nine initial visits, talked to twenty-seven alumni, and dialed 108 phone numbers.

The vast majority of this process will be invisible to you. Ask your development officer to complete this same exercise with you, filling in the numbers that correspond to the experience of your staff. This will give you a greater appreciation of how much work they do and a better understanding of how to motivate and reward them.

Here are some expectations you should have of your staff:

○ *They should identify opportunities*. They should bring you new ideas regularly for new development programs and strategies with individual donors.

○ *They should work independently*. You and your development officer should agree on a level of communication that will give you the assurance you need that work is happening without your looking over your development officer's shoulder every day.

○ *They should deploy you wisely*. You do not need to see every donor, and not every donor needs to see you. Once you give the staff your time, they should be sure that every minute of it is used to best possible advantage, doing things only you can do.

○ *They will tell you the unvarnished truth.* Especially if you are new to development, you will not get it right every time. Your development officer should be the person who closes the door and tells you, respectfully but candidly, how you are doing with donors.

What Your Development Staff Should Expect from You

You play a significant role in your development staff's productivity through direct work with donors. You also affect their ability to achieve their goals by the way you engage with them. Here are some of the expectations your staff should have of you:

○ *You should let your development team do their work.* If you constantly assign the development staff nondevelopment projects, they cannot raise money. They may be good at putting on events, but diverting them to plan the faculty retirement party is not going to help them achieve their annual goals.

○ *You should clearly communicate your unit's priorities.* Development officers need to be able to tell donors what really matters to you and to your program.

○ *You should keep them in the loop on significant developments.* Your chief development officer should sit in your cabinet of senior staff. This ensures that he or she will hear news, both good and bad, before donors do. Often your development staff will recognize opportunities in the general business of your program and can translate those into possibilities for donor engagement.

○ *You should be available and reliable.* Development work is not always efficient. It takes time to get to a donor meeting, spend meaningful time with a donor, and get back to campus. We recognize that your calendar is full of pressing engagements, and yet we need your time. The biggest gifts will not happen unless you devote significant time to your relationship with the donor.

Once you have committed your time, honor that commitment. One of a development officer's hardest phone calls is the one telling a potential donor that you have backed out of a visit. Of course, emergencies arise, but a budget meeting is not an emergency. Determine where development fits in your priorities, share that with the person who manages your calendar, and honor that priority.

○ *You should not shoot the messenger.* Sometimes your development staff has to bring you bad news. If you have messed up with a donor, your staff need to be able to tell you that without fear of losing their jobs. This speaks to the mutual trust that is an absolute requirement in these relationships. If your development staff are afraid you will punish them for bringing you bad news, they will avoid doing so. Your development performance will suffer as a result.

Performance Expectations

Unlike its partner programs, alumni relations and communications, fundraising is easily quantifiable. Good development officers are self-motivated. They thrive within a context of reasonable goals and targets.

Reasonable is the key word in this realm. Your officer's targets should reflect the nature of his or her assignments, the potential of your program, and the resources available to him or her. You and your fellow manager in the central development office are responsible for working with your officer to create this environment. Assigning targets that are impossible to reach within the capacity of your donor pool is a sure way to demoralize and drive away your development officer. Stretch goals are good motivators; impossible goals are not. Managing development officers is quite different from managing faculty. Your managerial partner in the development office has the experience to do this. He or she should guide you in assessing the appropriate targets for your officer—for example:

- Number of face-to-face visits

- Number of other donor contacts

- Number of new contacts attempted

- Number of new prospects identified

- Number of solicitations opened

- Number of solicitations closed

Portfolio factors should also be taken into account when establishing performance targets—for example:

- Proportion of time assigned to working directly on major gifts

- Number of additional development program responsibilities, such as annual giving or communications

- Proportion of time devoted to managing other staff

- Number of additional administrative responsibilities, such as data management or college committees

- The maturity of your program, as reflected in the officer's pool (the more mature the program, the more prospects; the newer the program, the more discovery work)

A major gift officer who has no other responsibilities should have a higher target for face-to-face visits than would your lead development officer. Your officer will carry a portfolio of donors, but also has to delegate time to staffing, working with faculty, and possibly managing other programs and staff. An officer who is working to identify new potential donors may have a high proportion of attempted contacts relative to face-to-face visits. An officer who has built or taken over a robust portfolio of well-qualified donors would have the reverse: significantly more face-to-face visits than cold calls.

You will notice that "dollars raised" is not on the list of targets. All of the other examples are activities your officer can control. The officer can make more calls, make more visits, open more solicitations, and so forth. But the officer cannot control the decisions donors make. Holding your officer accountable for other people's actions is unreasonable. Trust that if the officer is meeting all the other targets for good strategic activity, the money will follow.

Separate from their formal performance plan, most officers also want to set goals for how much money they will raise each year. It is also common for officers to set a target for themselves, such as raising a multiple of their salary. Over time, as the officer builds donor relationships and expands the capacity of the pool, this multiplier will rise. These types of goals can be motivational throughout the year and a source of great pride when the officer achieves the goals.

When discussing financial goals with your officer, remember that an officer can perform admirably in every way and yet not reach a dollar goal because a major donor's fortunes are reversed or the timing of a major prospect's giving changes.

Do not assign the officer the task of "covering" his or her own salary. Donors rarely want to designate their gifts to cover the salaries of those soliciting them. We always want development efforts to garner more than they cost, but making a direct link between gifts and pay creates an awkward dynamic between the solicitor and the solicited.

It is likely that your campus development program has established expectations in each of these areas. The expectations should be a range, with specific targets based on each officer's portfolio. Identifying the particular targets for your officer should be a collaborative effort among the officer, a development manager, and you. Each of you should contribute to a discussion of what would constitute ambitious but realistic targets, paying special attention to the officer's contributions to the discussion. A good officer knows the pool, knows the level of difficulty involved in engaging donors, and ultimately will be responsible for meeting the targets you jointly set.

Evaluating Performance

You and your officer should agree on a relatively simple method for evaluating progress toward targets throughout the year. This can probably be accomplished by reviewing standard reports the officer can retrieve from the central development database managers. Regular reviews, generally quarterly, give you peace of mind that the officer is continuing with the plans you have jointly made. It gives the officer an opportunity to show you the scope of work he or she is conducting, much of which happens outside your presence.

If the officer appears not to be making adequate progress toward targets, it is important to discuss why. Perhaps the new pool the officer is attempting to engage has proven more difficult to contact than expected. Perhaps there has been a staff resignation and the officer is temporarily bearing extra responsibilities in the office. Perhaps new projects have arisen that have taken the officer out of the field. Whatever the case, these quarterly check-ins provide an opportunity to discuss how to respond. In some cases, the targets should be adjusted downward to reflect what you and the officer have learned about realistic expectations for your pool. In others, the unexpected developments should be addressed. Where these developments involve assignments that are not fundraising related, you should take responsibility for assigning them elsewhere. Your officer will probably conduct a similar review with a manager in development, and it may be appropriate for the three of you to confer simultaneously.

With regular check-ins throughout the year, the actual performance evaluation should hold no surprises. You and the development manager should both participate in the performance evaluation meeting and documentation. This ensures that the officer gets consistent feedback from both managerial lines.

Rewarding and Retaining Development Officers

Development staff turnover is costly. There are expenses associated with searches and a risk that you will not be able to find an equally qualified candidate for the same salary you have been paying. There are opportunity costs as well: your program slows down when it is understaffed. Throughout this book, I acknowledge the long time line that is often needed to secure truly significant gifts. A development officer who works with a donor for many years of the relationship can develop trust and confidence from the donor that are instrumental in the execution of a major gift or several such gifts over multiple years. Retaining good development officers is an investment in your program.

The factors to consider when setting your development officer's salary are similar to those you consider when setting faculty salaries: experience, responsibilities, internal equity, and market equity. Numerous professional organizations conduct salary surveys, and market comparisons for your area should be relatively easy to find.

You may wish to use a higher salary to recruit a good candidate or reward and retain a development staff member with whom you are particularly satisfied. On occasion you will find resistance to this from your managerial colleagues in development based on internal equity issues. Your staff is a small component of a larger campus development community, and campus development leadership must maintain a culture of fairness and equity within that community. When individual units raise their officers' compensation above the norms for the campus community, internal competition can begin. It is not wise for the university to have deans and program heads creating the possibility of bidding wars with each other for development staff. If your staff are good, you will face stiff competition from other organizations that will want to recruit them away from you. Do not make this situation worse by creating the same pressures internally. Ask the development management to share with you the compensation range for development officers on campus, and then do your best to position your officer's salary appropriately within it.

It is not appropriate to pay development officers a commission on the funds they raise. In fact, accepting commissions is expressly forbidden in the ethics statements of the two main international professional associations for fundraisers: the Council for Advancement and Support of Education and the Association of Fundraising Professionals. Commission-based compensation encourages short-term closure, potentially at the expense of longer-term commitments.

Consider this scenario. A donor tells a college development officer, "I want to commit to the college's campaign. If I make that commitment now, I can afford to give $50,000, and I will consider that my entire campaign gift. But I'm exploring selling my company some time in the next three to five years. If I do, and if it's worth as much as I think it will be, I could potentially give more—as much as $1 million—as a part of my distribution from the sale."

A development officer who depends on commissions as a component of his or her compensation might be tempted to close the $50,000 gift now, not knowing whether he or she will still be employed by your university in three to five years, or whether the company sale will definitely happen, or whether the future gift would actually turn out to be larger than the $50,000 gift today. It is better for your program to wait, cultivate the relationship with the donor, and position itself to secure the larger gift. Do not put your development officer in the position of having to choose between what is best for himself or herself and what is best for your program.

In recent years, some development programs have begun using financial incentives as part of their officers' compensation packages. Unlike direct commissions, these incentives, usually in the form of financial bonuses, are tied to achieving a set of overall goals, often without including dollars raised. Some such plans award the incentives across an entire team if the team's goals are met. These programs are not yet widely adopted. Confer with your central development program to determine your university's philosophy and practice in this area.

The best way to avoid having to replace a good officer is to avoid losing the officer in the first place. In addition to reviewing progress toward targets and highlighting high and low points of the year, your annual performance evaluation should include a discussion of your officer's job satisfaction and future plans. Nonmonetary factors can significantly influence your officer's job satisfaction, and thus the officer's likelihood of staying with your program for an extended period of time.

The following sections set out some factors to consider that may help retain a good officer.

Environment

In Chapter Twenty-One, we discuss engaging your program's community in your development efforts. This includes creating a positive environment for the development staff. If it is common among faculty to make joking references about fundraising, such as, "Watch out! Here comes the development staff; hide your wallet," or to refer to fundraising as "picking pockets" or "twisting arms," the effect on your staff's morale can be significant. Fundraisers who feel respected by their community will be more satisfied and more likely to commit to your program for a longer tenure.

Self-Determination

Good fundraisers tend to be goal oriented. Mutually agreed-on goals that require hard work are generally a welcome motivator. Goals that are set arbitrarily and are regularly beyond the fundraiser's capacity to achieve have the opposite effect. Some programs assign goals to fundraisers based solely on the unit's needs, without regard for the giving capacity of the constituency or the stage of maturity of the program and its ability to produce significant results. Creating an environment where the fundraisers feel doomed to fail may drive them to seek a program where they can be part of setting program targets. Engage your development officer in conversations about goals. A good officer will not use this interaction to undercut targets or shirk responsibility for hard work.

Flexibility in Work Arrangements

Much of your development officer's work can be done anywhere—phoning for appointments, reviewing research, writing proposals, documenting visits. For some officers, implementing a flexible work schedule or a partial telecommuting arrangement can be as valuable as a salary increase. A clear understanding about this person's availability during flextime or telecommuting time, along with regular assessments of how the arrangement is working, can provide your officer with greater job satisfaction, with no detriment to program outcomes.

Professional Development Opportunities

Development is a constantly evolving field. Whether your officer has aspirations for career advancement or merely wants a fresh approach to standard components of his or her work, professional development opportunities can be an important component of a staff member's job satisfaction. Support your officer's interest in belonging to and volunteering for appropriate professional organizations. Confer with your managerial colleague in central development to determine appropriate on- or off-campus learning opportunities. Provide your officer with a small budget to attend at least one significant professional development activity each year.

Continued Education

Development officers who are drawn to work in universities value higher education. If your officer is thinking about graduate work, whether at the master's or doctoral level, you should support this interest. A continued commitment to education confirms the officer's credibility with faculty and provides a contact point with potential donors. Occasionally the officer will use this continued education to advance to a position in another organization. More often, the gratitude for support of this endeavor is poured back into the job, and the officer commits even more deeply to your cause.

3

Working with the Central
Development Office

W here your university falls on the centralized/decentralized spectrum (see Chapter Two) will determine the role the central development office will play in your development efforts. On the centralized end of the spectrum, the central office will likely exert significant authority over all development activities, including your own. On the other end of the spectrum, the central office may be merely a provider of infrastructure services to your program. Whatever your university's model, a good relationship with central development will benefit your program.

This successful relationship relies on your partnership with the chief development officer for the campus. As I suggested in the staffing structure discussion in Chapter Two, begin with an in-depth meeting with this person (generally the vice president for development or institutional advancement). Understanding the parameters within which the vice president works will help you understand how to get the most from this relationship. Some questions to ask:

- How are the campus's fundraising programs organized?

- Who are the key managers in the central development program?

- Who are the key volunteer leaders in the central development program?

- What are the campuswide fundraising goals, and how are they set?

- How is the development program evaluated?

- How is the vice president evaluated?

- What are the president's fundraising priorities?

- What is the vice president's philosophy toward fundraising?

- What does the vice president see as the university's biggest fundraising opportunities and challenges?

- What is the vice president's assessment of your program's development potential?

- What services does the central development program provide to the units?

- What are the university's prospect management policies and procedures?

- What other central policies and procedures are in place that the units must follow?

In addition to this initial fact-finding meeting, continue to meet on a somewhat regular basis with the vice president. He or she is a good source of information and guidance on how to improve your fundraising results.

Resources Available Through the Central Office

Regardless of where your campus program falls on the spectrum from centralized to decentralized, it is likely that the central development office has resources available to you.

Prospect Research

Gathering information about a donor's financial circumstances is immensely helpful in determining a solicitation strategy. The central office usually maintains a staff of researchers who have the skill sets necessary to ferret out information from sources that might never occur to you or your development officer.

Major Gift Officers

It is common for a university to have a team of major gift officers who are managed centrally and can develop donor relationships on behalf of any unit on campus. In many cases, these officers cover regional territories. Any one college may not have an adequate number of constituents in a region to justify the cost of a full-time development officer, yet the combination of all colleges may. You can use these officers as an extension of your own staffing.

Events

You can use centrally produced events as engagement opportunities for donors with whom you are working, usually at no cost to you.

Helping Central Development Succeed

A common misconception on campuses is that the central development office has a large portfolio of major donors who are ready to give and are merely waiting for the central office to tell them where they should designate their gifts. Nothing could be further from the truth. If those donors were truly ready to give, they would have done so by now. And when they do give, they will designate their gifts in accordance with their personal values, interests, and aspirations. While the central office can show these donors possibilities, they cannot control when, where, or how much the donors will give.

Most development staff and programs are judged by the results they achieve. In Chapter Nine, we look at creative ways to present academic programs in such a way that they align with potential donors' priorities. You can take the same approach with your campus development office. Determine what you have within your unit's development priorities that aligns with the overall campus goals. Offer to help the central office achieve its goals. For instance, if development has been told to secure twenty new endowed chairs over the next three years, a dean could share plans for establishing chairs within his or her college and the potential donors who might fund them. If scholarships are the top campus priority, show the vice president your goals for scholarships and what you plan to do to achieve them.

Remaining visible to the leadership of the central office is key to benefiting from their efforts:

- Ask to meet with the development management team and any centrally based fundraisers at least once or twice a year. Use these encounters to share what is happening in your program and to offer to work with them to raise funds.

- Attend centrally sponsored events with your donors.

- Provide content for their communications pieces.

- Acknowledge them when they have helped you. They have limited resources and many academic units. Show them the benefits of devoting their time to you.

The most significant obstacles to a good working relationship with the central development office tend to center around access to donors and potential donors. The process of determining and managing access is called *prospect management*. We look at this topic in depth in Chapter Four.

4

Prospect Management

Prospect management is the process by which a development program defines how it will interact with donors and prospective donors, oversees the application of guidelines regarding access to constituents, and tracks interactions with donors. Because it determines whether and how you can establish and develop relationships with potential supporters, it has significant ramifications for your program.

The term *prospect management* seems to imply that we are "managing" the prospects who may support our universities, but it is actually our relationships with these individuals that we are managing. In fact, some universities have begun replacing the traditional nomenclature with *relationship management*. Regardless of the formal name used, at their core, these systems are tools for us to manage ourselves and our own behavior toward supporters.

The foundation of a prospect management system is the university's philosophy on who can have access to and interactions with donors and potential donors. An effective prospect management system keeps the donor at the center of its focus. Approaches to donors are coordinated so that we consistently treat them with respect and show them how much we value their lifelong connection to our universities. Solicitation strategies center around what the donor wishes to accomplish, not what we most want. The university does not overwhelm donors with frequent overlapping approaches. Most important, an effective prospect management program never puts the donor in the position of having to adjudicate conflicting approaches from multiple units within a single university.

Prospect Management Roles

University personnel who are authorized to interact with a particular donor have assigned roles.

The *prospect manager* is the development staff member who takes the lead in the relationship, drives the strategy for engaging the constituent, and coordinates the activities of others in relation to this donor. This assignment is generally applied to constituents (the prospects) who have been determined to have significant likelihood of making a gift. Even after a donor has given, *prospect manager* remains the term used for the primary staff person in this relationship.

A *suspect manager* is similar to a prospect manager, but in this case it is not yet clear whether a particular constituent is a realistic prospect for a gift. In others words, we *suspect* that the constituent could become interested in giving, but there is much work to be done assessing the situation before we can be sure. Suspect managers attempt to establish contact with the constituent, with the intent of exploring whether the interest and capacity for significant giving exist.

The *staff* designation is assigned to development staff members who may know and interact with the constituent but are not actively driving the solicitation relationship. An example is an alumni relations staff member who works with the constituent in the context of a regional alumni club but does not have solicitation responsibilities.

A *natural partner* is someone who has a connection to the constituent and can advance the solicitation but is not on the development staff. Common natural partners are fellow volunteers and faculty with whom the donor has maintained a relationship. Your assignments will generally be in this category.

Decision Making and Control

Just as development organizational models range from centralized to decentralized, prospect management systems range from tightly controlled to loosely controlled.

In a tightly controlled prospect management environment, decisions about who works with which donors are made centrally. A central management team assesses prospective donors to determine where they are likely to direct their giving and who is best equipped to work with them to secure a gift. This team then assigns a staff member to serve as prospect manager and may also identify other university personnel in staff or natural partner roles. In these systems, anyone desiring to have contact with the donor must request and receive approval from the prospect manager. Tightly controlled systems often have a process by which planned solicitations must be proposed and approved before they can be implemented.

The most loosely controlled prospect management environment provides open access to all constituents by all university representatives. Prior approval for contact is not required, even for solicitations, though documentation of contacts after they have occurred is encouraged. If assignment terminology is used in this system, it is likely to be self-applied. The first staff member to discover a potential donor assigns himself or herself as prospect manager without a formal request or approval process.

Along the spectrum between these two extremes are many variations in prospect management systems. In these in-between environments, the management team has approval authority but is primarily reactive, not proactive. Staff members are expected to request assignments, providing a rationale for why they should take on each role. Others who wish to contact prospects are required to notify the prospect manager of their interest. The prospect manager is expected not to obstruct such contact unless a specific gift negotiation is under way. In that case, the contact should be delayed until the discussions have concluded.

Your development officer or the central development office can help you determine the degree of control inherent in your university's approach and provide you with your campus's prospect management policies and procedures. The policy generally addresses these topics:

- The university's philosophy toward relationships with donors

- Your university's specific prospect management terminology, such as *prospect manager, suspect manager, staff,* or *natural partner*

- Who makes decisions about prospect management assignments

- The process for requesting prospect management assignments

- Responsibilities associated with each type of assignment

- Methods for documenting and tracking donor interactions

Your development officer should have been provided with training in how the process works and can brief you on how it affects your activities. More often than not, a potential donor who has a preexisting affiliation with your program, and whose interests indicate likelihood of supporting your program, will be assigned to your development officer, or to a centrally based officer with whom your officer works closely. The more complex assignments arise when a donor is interested in several areas. We look at that coordination process in Chapter Twenty.

Challenges

It is not uncommon for academic leaders to grow frustrated with centralized prospect management systems. It can be irritating to have to go through a process when you are confident that a potential donor has no other interests on the campus and that you and your development officer are the appropriate contacts for the prospect. It can be even more distressing when the system does not play out in your favor. As frustrating as it can be to have your access to a potential supporter restricted, complying with prospect management decisions is important. Circumventing the process has the potential to create inappropriate encounters with donors for you, for the assigned staff, and for other academic representatives who engage with the constituent.

Imagine the awkwardness of a dean who is assigned to a relationship's arriving for a visit only to learn that another dean has visited the donor on another matter the day before. The assigned dean is now in the embarrassing position of appearing not to know what his or her colleagues are doing. More significant, it conveys to the donor that the university does not coordinate its actions and that internal communication is inadequate. If a university cannot manage those basic activities, why should the donor think that the university can manage the much more complex task of properly stewarding a major gift?

Knowing what role your officer plays in the prospect management decision-making process, and respecting that role, are important. Do not ask your officer to circumvent the decisions that have been made, even if you strongly disagree with them. Your officer needs to maintain good relationships with the development community on your campus in order to have access to the resources he or she needs to be successful on your behalf.

Prospect Management Matters

Disregarding prospect management is a cardinal sin among good development officers. Whatever short-term gain you may feel you have accomplished by expecting your officer to circumvent the system will likely be eclipsed by negative consequences over the long term.

When you and your officer are denied an assignment to a prospect with whom you feel confident you should be engaged, there are several constructive steps you can take:

- *Appeal the decision.* Your prospect management system may have a process for reconsidering decisions. If so, follow it thoughtfully. Provide a thorough rationale for your involvement with the prospect. Unless the assignment is outrageously inappropriate, request to be added to the assignment team, not to replace the established assignment. This avoids putting the decision makers into a position of having to admit a mistake to accommodate your request.

- *Go to the top.* This can be a topic of conversation in one of your regular meetings with the campus's chief development officer. Respectfully request an explanation of the rationale for the decision. The decision may not be reversed, but you will have shown that you take these matters seriously and are assertive in advancing your college's interests. You will have gained perspective that may help you and your officer present future requests in more persuasive ways. Be careful not to put your officer at risk in this conversation. Emphasize to the chief development officer that you were not dispatched by your officer to undermine the authority of the decision makers. You are merely gathering information in order to be more effective in your future endeavors.

- *Attempt a collaboration.* You and your officer can contact your colleagues who have been given the assignment and request to work together. As we will see in Chapter Twenty, this approach can be appealing if it expands and deepens the prospect's relationship with the university.

If you have not been given responsibility for one of your major donors, find ways to maintain your relationship with the prospect without violating the assignment decision. You and your development officer should confer with the assigned staff and with development management to determine what is appropriate. You may be able to invite the prospect to attend events or continue his or her engagement in a volunteer activity. Whatever you agree on, do not overstep the bounds of the agreement. Use the continued contact to deepen the prospect's interest in your program, but do not take the step of asking for a gift. Over time, the prospect may decide to support your program in spite of, or in addition to, the focus of the other area. Once the primary assigned staff have implemented their solicitation, the ground will be laid for you and your officer to request that you take the lead on the next round of engagement.

5

Organizing Your Time for Development Success

Your development colleagues are well aware that the demands on your time are vast and varied. When you dedicate a portion of your time to development, it is their responsibility to help you use that time strategically.

Priorities

A typical classification of development priorities for an academic leader involves three categories:

A Level

- Relationships with your program's highest-level prospects and donors, including initial connections, cultivation, solicitation, and stewardship

- Setting your college's development priorities

- Consulting with your development staff on program strategies

B Level

- Adding your personal voice and style to annual giving and other messages

- Attending events

- General donor relations

C Level

- Gift processing

- Writing mailings and phone scripts

- Prospect research

- Cold calls to low-level prospects or suspects

To be successful, you *must* invest time in the A-level priorities, and you *should* invest time in the B-level priorities. You should never spend time on the C-level priorities, because this is work that development staff should do.

Time

Senior academics who are superstar fundraisers spend more than half their time on development. They are, however, very rare. Achieving this level of engagement requires significant investment in an administrative infrastructure that ensures the smooth operation of the program while the academic is engaged in external work. In most cases, this has been built incrementally over many years.

If you are just beginning your work in development, commit to spending at least 3 to 5 percent of your time in this area. If you are already devoting some time, considering increasing that amount by one or two percentage points each year until you have reached a level that is producing good results for your program without creating unmanageable burdens internally.

Finding the Time

Start with a time audit. Document how you are spending your time, both on campus and off. Assess each responsibility, and consider whether it is important and whether you are the only one who can handle it.

Confer with your unit's management team to ensure that routine tasks and procedures are actually necessary. Some may be traditions that no longer serve an important purpose. You may also find that some of these tasks are being done for other areas of the university. As you discuss your development plans with your provost or other manager, consider negotiating out of some of his or her required routine processes in order to spend more time generating income through development.

Internally, you may be able to delegate tasks that are time-consuming but only moderately important to other members of your team. Assignments that are routine for you can be growth opportunities for faculty and other administrators who are interested in expanding their experience.

Externally, be sure that each commitment you undertake is contributing to the advancement of either your college or your own career. Some of these external commitments may hold development possibilities that your staff can help you pursue. For example, civic clubs and organizations provide entrée to leaders in your community, and you may cultivate the connections you develop with them into volunteering for or giving to your program.

Your assistant is a vital member of the development team and plays a crucial role in making time available for your fundraising work. Convey to your assistant the level of priority that you are placing on development activities, so that he or she does not preempt them for lower-priority internal activities. Allow your assistant and your development officer to collaborate on scheduling your development time.

In addition to organizing your calendar to make time available, your assistant serves as a primary point of interaction with other administrative professionals on your donors' staffs. Your assistant's good relationships with these contacts can significantly improve the chances that you and your donors will be able to find time in

your equally busy schedules to have the encounters that are necessary in building an engaged relationship.

Using Development Time Strategically

In the early stages of your development work, what you are doing
is much more important than how often you are doing it. Confer
with your development officer to create a list of action items.
Include activities that can be addressed when small windows of
time present themselves (thank-you calls for recent gifts) and
those that require large blocks of time (a trip to a region where
you have a strong constituency).

Once you and your officer have agreed on this list, allow your
officer to begin implementing the main items. For example, commit
to a set number of specific lunch times over the next two months.
Have your development officer contact high-priority donors and
prospects to fill the slots. Engage your assistant in keeping the less
time-consuming tasks in mind during your in-office time.

As you work through the list, you and your assistant should
communicate back to the development staff about both what you
have done and the content of these actions. The development staff
will add that information to the ongoing documentation of the
university's relationships with these individuals.

This to-do list should be the main agenda item for your
regular meetings with your development officer. The two of you
should review the list, reassess priorities, discuss any obstacles
that have arisen, and debrief on outcomes. As assignments are
completed, add new ones, always maintaining a robust list of
responsibilities.

Honoring Your Time Commitment

In the crush of your daily responsibilities, along with the regular
crises that reach your office, it can be tempting to push your development work lower and lower on your priority list. This is a
mistake. When you have committed time to development, honor

it. Require that your development staff ensure that the time will be well spent and productive.

Sending the Right Messages to Donors

The biggest and best gifts to your program will not happen without your presence. Communicating, either overtly or through inattention, that you do not consider these gifts a high priority will undermine your development program's outcomes and will convey a chilling message to your donors. Remember that donors are as busy as you are. If they are willing to take time out of their responsibilities to commune with you, you should be willing to do the same.

Part Two

Development Basics from an Academic Leader's Perspective

6

The Cycle of Giving

A significant gift is rarely a freestanding occurrence. It generally happens in the midst of a continuum that we hope will extend and repeat itself over a long period of time as our relationship with the donor evolves and the donor gives again and again. Development professionals commonly refer to this continuum as the cycle of giving. The stages of giving are

Identification ⟶ Qualification ⟶ Cultivation ⟶ Solicitation ⟶ Stewardship

Identification

The giving continuum begins with the identification of a potential donor. This step is usually undertaken by the development staff. They reach out to many potential donors through general means, such as direct mail and communication pieces, and through individualized means, such as personal e-mail messages or phone calls, attempting to secure a visit.

The goal of the identification process is to sift through large quantities of data and find the small portion of your constituency with three key characteristics:

- They have the capacity to give a significant gift.

- They have charitable inclinations.

- They are, or could be, favorably disposed to your institution.

Without all three of those characteristics present, it is unlikely the constituent will ever make a major gift to your program.

To identify these potential givers, development staff look at numerous indicators:

- Signs of wealth—for example, living in a wealthy area; significant stock holdings disclosed to the Securities and Exchange Commission; or ownership of high-value real assets, such as art collections or yachts, or ownership of multiple properties

- Business successes such as salary level, ownership of a business, or appointments to corporate boards

- Prior giving to your institution

- Giving patterns to other institutions

- Media coverage

- Engagement with your institution through volunteer activities

- Demonstrated interest in other programs like yours

- An indication that an individual's personal values have a strong alliance with your program's mission

When the development officer identifies someone who might become a significant donor, the process of attempting to establish contact and secure a personal visit begins. It is uncommon for academics to be directly involved in the identification stage. For the most part this is a game of numbers, as we explored in Chapter Two, and it is best handled by development professionals.

There are two main exceptions to this practice. The first is potential donors whom you know personally—perhaps alumni of your program or people with whom you have connected through professional circles. In this case, a query from you to request a visit is a natural extension of your existing relationship.

The second is potential donors who are unlikely to respond to a development officer because of their social, economic, or professional status. It can be difficult for a development officer to break through the many layers of gatekeepers who surround people of high status. Your title carries more weight than your development officer's. Some people in these high-status categories may wish to interact only with someone of similar status. In the academy, that may be you.

Friend or Donor?

Academics often ask whether they should attempt to engage a personal friend who is wealthy. The bonds of friendship do not always carry over from the emotional relationship into a financial one. Only you can assess whether your relationship is strong enough to withstand the potential awkwardness if you approach your friend about giving and the friend declines. Often the best approach is a direct question: "Would it be okay for me to tell you about my college's financial needs and explore whether you might be interested in giving to the program?" If your friend responds favorably, by all means continue the conversation and move toward a solicitation. If your friend demurs, shelve the idea. It is possible that he or she will develop an interest in the future and will approach you then to restart the conversation. Let that be the friend's choice.

Qualification

Once contact has been made and the potential donor has agreed to a visit, the development officer moves into the stage known as *qualification*. In this stage, we are attempting to learn enough about the donor to know whether this person is qualified to make a significant gift. We need to know whether this person meets the three key characteristics already mentioned. Sometimes we can tell in a first meeting whether this is the case:

- The individual expresses great affinity for the university and has obvious wealth.

- The individual is clearly of modest means and thus may be at most a donor to the annual fund at this time.

- There may be adequate wealth to indicate the potential of a large gift, but not soon. Perhaps the individual has children who are not yet on their own or wealth that is tied up in illiquid form.

In each of these cases, the development officer can fairly easily determine a strategy for proceeding. When the answer is not as obvious, the development officer will attempt to secure a second visit in order to gain more information. Good development officers are excellent listeners and have a bevy of questions they use to elicit information about the individual's likelihood of becoming a donor.

By the end of the second visit, we almost always know how we should proceed. For those who are unlikely to be major donors, we continue the relationship through general communications. We may visit again from time to time to determine whether a person's circumstances have changed. This individual will not be a major focus for the development officer's time and probably will not be included on your visit list.

For those who do seem to have both the potential and the interest that indicate the possibility of a donor relationship, we move into the cultivation stage.

Cultivation

This is the process by which we cultivate a relationship with an individual who may become a major donor to our program. It used to be common for development professionals to refer to cultivation as if it were something we do to our potential donors: "I'm cultivating Mr. Jones for a gift." A more contemporary way of thinking recognizes that our donors are not fields to be tilled. Rather, it is the relationship between the donor and the institution that should be fed, nurtured, and encouraged to grow. A careful investment in developing an engaged relationship will set the stage for a successful solicitation later on.

Development professionals move smoothly from the qualification to the cultivation stage, often within the same meeting. We continue to ask questions and listen carefully to what we are hearing. Whereas the qualification stage is concluded in one or two visits, the cultivation stage is unpredictable. Occasionally donors are ready to give, and we can move to solicitation quickly. More often, it takes months, or even years, to move through this stage.

The cultivation stage is where academic leaders are most likely to enter the relationship. While getting to know a prospective donor, development officers explore a wide range of topics. Much of this discovery is oriented toward understanding how the potential donor makes giving decisions. During this part of the process, a development officer assesses whether you should be involved in this relationship. Perhaps the donor wants a sense of the leadership of the program, or the potential gift is large enough that you would need to take a hand in managing the outcomes.

At this point, the development officer arranges a visit for you to meet with the potential donor, usually with the development officer present as well. From this point forward, you are developing a partnership with this donor. This partnership will result in the donor's becoming engaged with your program at a level where he or she is deeply invested in its and your success. That is what leads to extraordinary gifts. Chapters Eight and Nine go into detail on how to establish yourself in the relationship and use this process strategically to prepare for solicitation.

If cultivation can take anywhere from a few visits to several years, how do we know when the relationship has progressed to the point where it's time to move into the solicitation stage? The guideline is, if both you and the donor are ready to discuss a gift, then it is time to move on to the solicitation. If either of you is not ready, cultivation should continue.

Solicitation

Though we often talk about "a" solicitation as if it were a discrete act, most solicitations for large gifts extend over a series of conversations. These conversations translate the donor's desire for your program to succeed into concrete action he or she can take to ensure this success. When the engagement between the donor and the university is strong and well developed, the solicitation phase will be a natural and easy one.

Chapter Ten explores the solicitation process in depth. For now, keep in mind that giving is a natural step in the relationships you are building with your program's friends. It is a process that both you and the donor can enjoy immensely. And the end result is nothing less than thrilling.

Stewardship

Once the solicitation has concluded and the gift has been secured, the relationship is far from over. During this stewardship stage, we are stewarding several things: the gift the donor has given, the relationship we have with the donor, and the trust the donor has shown in us by making the gift. Most development professionals have encountered donors who are hesitant to commit to a gift because they are concerned that once the gift has been made, we will stop visiting them. We must convey to our donors that we view this as a lifelong relationship. Although the nature of our conversations may change, we will stay in touch and continue to nurture the relationship out into the future.

The stewardship stage provides the opportunity to show donors the impact of their gift. This is often a dream come true for donors, and it is exciting to be part of it. We are also showing them that we are trustworthy guardians of their gift and confirming that their choice to support us was a wise one. The logistical components of stewardship are addressed in Chapter Eleven.

Our relationships with donors deepen even further in the stewardship stage. You will be a part of joyful moments with them as they experience what their gift has accomplished, and as they see how carefully you use their gift, they will come to trust you even more. Over time, it is not uncommon for new gift ideas to emerge. Sometimes donors want to do more of what they originally did: increase the number of students receiving their scholarships or renovate a second space, for example. Other times, as they learn even more about your program as they watch their gift in action, they notice other areas that catch their interest.

This is the point where stewardship seamlessly evolves back into cultivation. This time the relationship is already well established. What is being cultivated is a new facet to the relationship, a new opportunity. On our continuum, we now draw a loop back around to the cultivation stage, and the process of moving toward solicitation begins again.

Over time we may go through this cycle with a donor many times. Consider the life span of your alumni. They may have a sixty- or seventy-year relationship with your institution. During that long relationship, there will be many opportunities for them to invest, and they may give gifts of various types and sizes. If we are careful stewards of our relationships over decades, we will see larger and larger gifts as our partnerships mature.

Before we focus on the specifics of your involvement with donors, we look at the different ways people give and how those work together in your program.

7

Types of Giving

Just as there is a continuum in giving relationships, there is a continuum in types of gifts.

Annual Gifts ⟶ Major Gifts ⟶ Principal Gifts ⟶ Planned Gifts

Some donors move sequentially along the continuum, some jump around between types of giving, and others give in multiple ways simultaneously. Ascertaining which type of gift will be most appealing to a donor is an important part of planning for a successful solicitation.

Annual Gifts

Annual gifts are, as the term implies, renewable. They are small in size, within the donor's capacity. Remember that to the very wealthy, a six-figure gift may not feel large. Due to their relatively low dollar amount, annual gifts are generally grouped together to accomplish a programmatic purpose. The amalgamation of these gifts is commonly referred to as the *annual fund*.

A key difference between an annual gift and a major gift is the donor's decision-making process. An annual gift tends to be somewhat transactional: the appeal is straightforward, and the investment is moderate. Most donors do not go through a complex and involved decision-making process when determining whether to make an annual gift. Think of your own charitable giving. You probably receive appeals from a variety of organizations, sort through them and save the ones in which you have an interest, then decide how to divide your charitable dollars among them. Most of us make these decisions in the context of paying our bills. Annual gifts are usually made from discretionary cash, not through liquidation of a significant asset.

Smaller gifts tend to be given without significant restriction and are generally applied to operating costs. Some universities encourage low-level donors to give to a single pool of gifts, a university-wide unrestricted annual fund. Others follow the donors' interests by establishing annual funds within each of their programs. Although these gifts are restricted to a particular unit, they are unrestricted within that unit. In either case, the head of the benefiting program has the discretion to determine how the funds should be used.

Most annual gifts are solicited through broad vehicles such as direct mail, telemarketing, and e-solicitations. Targeting and implementing these solicitations is a complicated process, fueled by market research and careful analysis of programs' results.

For some donors, annual giving represents the extent of their giving potential. For others, annual giving is the first step on a ladder of increasingly large gifts. As donors increase their annual gifts, we move into a more personal approach. Development officers often contact these donors to renew, and attempt to increase, their giving. These contacts have a dual purpose: in addition to ensuring a continued flow of unrestricted dollars to the program, they give the officers an opportunity to assess whether these donors have the capacity to make larger gifts. If they do, the officer begins the process of moving toward a larger solicitation.

Lower-level donors may feel concerned that their small gifts are irrelevant in a large program. It is incumbent on us to show them the impact of their giving, combined with the gifts of many other donors like them. If you have the discretion to determine how your annual fund is spent, direct it to discrete purposes, not just into a general operating fund. Telling donors that their gifts were used to support faculty travel, or scholarships, or student organizations helps them see the impact even a small gift can make. The more relevant a donor feels, the more likely that person is to make another gift.

Annual giving programs often include giving societies that usually have an overall name, along with names at various giving levels. These societies are a donor recognition tool that I discuss in greater detail in Chapter Fourteen.

Major Gifts

Most development programs define a major gift by a dollar amount appropriate to their program. This can range from $1,000 in nascent programs to $100,000 or more in robust, well-established programs. The dollar amount is usually determined based on the range of gifts the program can expect in a year and the size of gift that stands out as more significant than the average gift. The designation of "major" indicates that donors whose next gift is likely to be at or above this level will be approached in a more personal, targeted way than are donors below this level.

While the definition of *major gift* can be a helpful organizational tool, it is important to keep in mind that donors have their own opinions about what is major for them. A helpful distinction is the stop-and-think criterion: if the donor has to stop and think, this is probably a major gift. The stop-and-think process might include:

- Taking some time to determine whether a gift of this size is possible

- Involving multiple decision makers, such as the donor's spouse, children, or financial advisers

- Wanting to explore various designations for the gift and the impact the gift would have in each of these areas

- Researching the program's accomplishments to
  determine whether this is a reliable investment

To a donor, a major gift is an unusual occurrence. Some donors make only one major gift in their entire lifetime. Others may give multiple major gifts, but these are generally spaced out with multiyear intervals between them. Unlike with the transactional nature of annual gifts, major gifts involve a more complex relationship between the donor and the beneficiary. The larger the gift, the more involved this relationship will be. The process of securing such a gift can take months or years, with multiple conversations among multiple parties over time. In subsequent chapters, we explore these relationships in depth.

Because a major gift is almost always designated for a specific purpose, both sides of the relationship have greater expectations for the outcome of the gift. While an annual gift is easily documented with a simple reply device and a corresponding financial transfer, a major gift usually includes written agreements between the donor and the institution. The gift agreement should address the amount of the gift, the terms under which it will be fulfilled, how it will be used, and how the donor will be kept informed about its use. This also creates greater expectations of continued communication from the program to the donor. While annual donors may receive a single mass communication regarding the impact of the annual fund in a given year, major donors should receive individualized communications regarding their gifts. If the gift was to endowment, these communications will continue in perpetuity.

Larger gifts often bring public recognition through the naming of a building or a space within it or the naming of a fund that is acknowledged whenever the fund is used. There may be a ceremony to announce the gift. There is often a communications plan that includes a press release and stories about the gift in your own publications. Depending on the size of the gift, the prominence of your program, and the stature of the donor, there may be media coverage.

Principal Gifts

The term *principal gift* refers to a very large major gift. Most institutions, and the development field at large, consider a principal gift to be $5 million or more. In recent years, we have seen a number of extraordinarily large gifts to higher education, at the $100 million level and higher. The amount for programs that are just getting established in their development work is lower. In your own program, a principal gift is one that is transformational in nature.

Everything described in the section on major gifts is true of principal gifts, but greatly amplified. Using a gift of this size properly takes a great deal of internal discussion and strategic thinking. A rare opportunity like this should be approached carefully and thoughtfully to ensure that the donor has the impact he or she desires and that the program benefits permanently from the infusion of this level of funding.

Principal gift donors have generally been engaged with the organization for years and have often given numerous smaller gifts. We all love the stories of the serendipitous arrival of a giant check from a previously unknown friend. The reality is that almost every gift at this level is the result of many years of investment on both sides of the relationship. This level of support requires an absolute match of values between the donor and the program and is usually the culmination of a lifetime of shared experiences.

You will sometimes hear the term *ultimate gift* within the context of principal gift discussions. The ultimate gift is exactly what the term implies: the final gift that will cap off the donor's support of your program. It may be a single gift secured in the donor's estate plan or a package of gifts to be made over a number of years. Ultimate gifts grow out of the donors', or donor families', consideration of what they want their permanent legacy to be within your institution. This elevates their thinking out of considering one project at a time and into a bigger view of their hopes and dreams for your program and for their impact on it.

Planned Gifts

Planned giving is the component of a development program that deals with estate plans and income-producing gift vehicles. It is a technique for giving that can be used at the major or principal gift level. Planned giving programs provide donors with financial options that can often make it possible for them to give larger gifts than they could make out of their current assets.

This is a specialized field with many technical and legal requirements. Good planned giving practitioners have years of education in this area and participate in ongoing professional development to stay abreast of tax law changes and new financial devices. Your central development office probably has at least one planned giving expert. If a donor mentions estate planning or bequests or has questions regarding how to coordinate giving to your program with providing for his or her family, a planned giving officer can help you move this conversation forward.

Do not go very far into a planned giving discussion unless you have significant technical training in this area. These vehicles have significant financial and legal ramifications for your institution. Those of us who are not proficient in this area should not take the risk of making commitments that would be disadvantageous to our organizations.

Gift Planning

Some planned giving professionals have begun to refer to their field as *gift planning*. This subtle change conveys their role in helping donors plan and implement their giving goals. Gift planning professionals can help donors with complicated stock transactions, gifts of real property, complex trust arrangements, and a host of other financial tools. They often work in tandem with other development officers, providing the technical expertise to assist donors in fulfilling a commitment that the other officer has solicited.

8

Stepping into a Donor Relationship

By the time a development officer asks you to meet with a potential donor, the officer will have already begun the relationship. He or she will have determined that a meeting between you and the prospect will move the relationship forward in significant ways.

Categorizing Donors

Over time you will meet a lot of donors, volunteers, and potential donors. As the number of your contacts grows, it can be helpful to categorize them:

- Your A list should consist of top donors and prospects who have significant gift potential. These should be relationships where the gift will not happen without your direct involvement.

- Your B list should comprise important donors and prospects who will benefit from your relationship but whose gift can be closed as effectively by someone else (generally the development officer).

- Your C list is your general college constituency, donors and nondonors alike, whom you will encounter in group settings or in casual interactions.

When you commit time to development visits, your development officer should ensure you spend your time almost exclusively on A list and B list relationships. If that is not happening, talk to your development officer about your program's overall population of donors and prospects. It may be that there are not yet very many major gift donors. If there are and your officer is not engaging you with them, you need to find the reason and resolve it.

You Have to Start Somewhere

New deans and program heads often tell us, "I don't want to go on any visit where I won't be closing a million dollar gift." Our reply is, "Okay, then you don't need to devote much time to this."

It takes time for relationships to progress. If your program is relatively new, you may have to spend time visiting with lower-level donors until you and your development officer have built a portfolio of significant givers. Stick with it: persistence is a virtue in this field.

Initial Visits

Your first visit with a potential major donor will set the tone for the rest of the relationship. If you relax and focus on the donor, you will be off to a great start.

The donor will be looking forward to this meeting. When we tell a potential donor, "The dean would like to meet you," the donor is honored and delighted. To a donor who does not work in academia, a senior academic administrator is an exalted figure. The donor may not have met a dean, a provost, or any senior administrator in person when he or she was a student at your institution. Your title provides you an entrée that sets the meeting up to go well.

Before you go on the visit, make sure you know why you are seeing this person. If your development officer has developed a sense of the long-term strategy for this relationship, discuss what that is and how your first visit can help advance it. Your development officer can also tell you if there is anything you need to know about the donor, particularly if there are sensitive topics you should avoid. Try not to overbrief yourself about the donor's life and circumstances. Knowing a little but not too much positions you to ask questions and learn about the donor in his or her own words.

It is best to have your development officer accompany you on this visit because this person is the common connection you and the donor have, and his or her presence will make the start of the meeting go more smoothly. You may find that you and your development officer hear things differently, or each of you may pick up on something the other misses.

Be sure that you, or your staff, have confirmed the logistics of the visit before you start out. Know how to get to the visit site and where to park. Get to the location at least ten minutes early, and use this cushion to go over your strategy before you enter the meeting location. Making a donor wait because you are late is not a good start to a long-term friendship.

Because the purpose of this first meeting is to get acquainted, do not feel pressured to accomplish much movement in the relationship. Definitely do not solicit a gift. You and the donor need to get to know each other and develop a comfortable rapport before you transact any business.

There is not even a need for you to initiate any conversation about fundraising during this first meeting. The person you are visiting will know that solicitation will be a part of your relationship at some point. Anyone who can afford to make a major gift has probably been solicited by many other causes. If the donor brings it up, do not be concerned about acknowledging that part of the relationship. Say that while you hope to count on his or her support, right now you are just focused on getting to know him or her.

As you are learning about the donor, it is okay to share bits of information about yourself and your program as well. A brief overview of recent accomplishments in your program can help the donor feel more connected to it. But do not go into great depth on any one topic unless it is clear from the donor's questions that he or she wants that level of detail. If all goes well, you will have numerous future opportunities to talk. You do not have to share everything on this first visit.

As this initial visit winds to a close, lay the groundwork for your next encounter with the potential donor. Stay alert for cues that will help you propose an appropriate next step. Your development officer may suggest a campus visit or some other engagement. Follow that lead and express how interested you are in continuing this relationship.

Close the visit by thanking the donor for his or her time. Articulate what will happen next: perhaps you will be sending the donor some additional information on a topic you discussed or your development officer will be getting in touch to schedule a visit.

Once the visit has concluded, debrief with your development officer about what you learned. While the meeting is fresh in your mind, assess what happened, and talk about what your short-term strategy should be. Make notes about specific next steps, and be sure to implement them.

Now that you have had your first visit, the relationship can begin to move purposefully toward solicitation.

Sample Follow-Up Steps to Keep a Relationship Moving Forward

- Send a packet of material targeted to interests that the donor identified in your meeting. Include a handwritten note thanking the donor for the visit.

- Invite the donor to attend a campus event as your guest. This need not be an event specific to your program. Athletic and cultural events provide opportunities for establishing rapport with donors.

- Suggest a meeting with a faculty member the donor has mentioned favorably. Ideally this meeting will happen on campus to give you an opportunity to show the donor your facilities and plans.

9

Cultivation

If your initial visit with a potential donor was successful, both you and the donor will be interested in continuing the relationship and getting to know each other better. This will be accomplished in the cultivation phase.

As I noted in the overview of the giving cycle in Chapter Six, cultivation is a two-way process. While we are getting to know the potential donor and exploring the possibility of securing a gift, the donor is getting to know our institution and is also exploring giving possibilities. An effective cultivation period allows both of us to get the information we need to make a decision about our potential partnership. This process is most successful when there is a free flow of information between the parties, each learning about the other's values, priorities, aspirations, and preferences.

There are infinite variations on how a relationship can develop. Your goal is to ensure that your relationships with prospective donors develop into partnerships that will result in the donors' investing in your program. Along the way, you may develop friendships or find other meaningful components to your relationship. No matter how worthwhile these additional facets may be, do not lose sight of your ultimate goal: soliciting a gift.

Understanding Donors

To develop a cultivation strategy, we must first be clear on what will be required for the donor to make a significant gift. Think about your own charitable giving. You may support a wide array of organizations, and you probably give more to some than to others. Consider why you make those larger gifts:

- Are those organizations closer to your heart?

- Do you have a longer relationship with them?

- Do you care more about what they do?

- Do you know more about them and thus have a better sense of what your gift will accomplish?

Some donors give for practical or self-oriented reasons, such as to receive tangible benefits or public recognition. But you will find that most give their truly significant gifts to programs that have captured their heart and their imagination. They give to help, to have an impact, to solve a problem that concerns them. They give to feel the happiness and satisfaction that come from accomplishing something that matters deeply to them. When you read the news coverage of a massive gift to an institution, the donors almost always talk about how good the gift made them feel and how important it was to them to help the institution they support. Giving is a powerful emotional experience for donors.

Your goal in cultivation is to tap into those emotions and discover how you can help the donor have that experience. Before you can show donors how your program could help them feel that good, you have to know what would work for them, what their values are, and what they aspire to accomplish with their giving.

This means a lot of talking about them before you talk about your program. If you are new to individual fundraising, this may seem out of kilter for you. Your experience in securing funding throughout your academic career has probably consisted almost entirely of talking about your work, its importance, and its relevance. Funding agencies do not make their decisions based on emotion. You read the guidelines, construct your proposal accordingly, and submit. You would not submit a grant without ensuring that your proposal was structured exactly the way the funding agency wanted it and included everything that agency wanted to see. So too we should not solicit individuals without first understanding what they want and then using that information to determine how to structure and present a request. In the world of individual giving, exploring the donor's emotions, values, and motivations is the equivalent of reading the guidelines.

What to Accomplish During Cultivation

There are also tangible pieces of information we want to gain while cultivating a donor relationship. A number of key questions need answers before we can expect a solicitation to be successful:

- What is the donor's giving capacity?

- What type of gift is the donor likely to make: one relatively quickly or one in the more distant future?

- How does the donor make giving decisions?

- Will this be an individual decision, or will others be involved in it?

- Is the donor ready to make a major commitment?

- What does the donor need to know to make a decision about giving?

- What are the donor's expectations once he or she has made a gift?

And the most important item of all:

- What component of our program will meet all of his or her emotional and practical motivations?

Meanwhile, the donor is gathering information as well. He or she may be attempting to determine answers to a number of questions:

- Is this academic a reliable and capable leader for the program?

- Is the program going in a direction I feel comfortable supporting?

- Are there program goals and realistic plans for meeting those goals?

- Will my money be properly managed?

- Can I be confident my gift will be used for the purpose I designate?

- Is this program important to the academic, and is the unit important to the university?

- How stable is the program? If the academic leaves, will my area of interest still be a priority?

- How much can my gift accomplish? Will it be enough to make an actual difference?

- Do I feel comfortable talking about financial issues with these people?

This mutual exploration process will take place over weeks, months, or years in the context of numerous encounters, such as meetings, meals, campus visits, e-mail exchanges, and phone conversations.

Purposeful Cultivation

Most development officers have experienced the phenomenon of endless cultivation. Relationships with donors can fall into a routine of regular encounters—often a lunch when we are in the donor's area—where the friendship between the institution and the donor is nurtured but no solicitation ever happens. Sometimes the routine becomes so well established that introducing a solicitation would be jarring. Other times the donor deftly avoids the solicitation frequently enough that it no longer seems appropriate to try again. Endless cultivation is much easier to prevent than to resolve.

The concept of purposeful cultivation helps us keep in mind that we are nurturing this relationship for a reason. Our end purpose—to secure a gift—should drive our strategies and our actions. If it does, the cultivation process will move more quickly and more effectively toward a solicitation.

To achieve your overall strategy of successful solicitation, you need to take a strategic approach to each encounter with the prospective donor. Before your meeting, determine what you want to learn and share in this discussion. Confer with your development officer to consider what pieces of information you still need to know and assess what you think the donor will want to know.

A good way to focus your strategy for a single encounter is to ask yourself, "Am I going to ask for a gift today?" Through the majority of the cultivation phase, the answer will be no. Then ask yourself, "Why not?" The reason may involve your readiness:

- "I don't know how much she would be able to give."

- "I haven't narrowed down which area he really wants to support."

- "We hardly know each other, and it would seem awkward to solicit this early."

Or it could involve the prospect's readiness:

- He hasn't indicated an area of interest.

- She still seems to have a lot of questions about the state of the program.

- They've mentioned their pledge to another institution and how they need to pay that off before making another commitment.

If you can articulate the reason that it is not time to solicit, you have also articulated a valid strategy for this visit. Plan your agenda around addressing one or more of the unresolved areas. Then you can be confident you will end the visit one step closer to solicitation.

After every encounter, reflect, synthesize, and plan. This is best done in conversation with your development officer, whether you both were part of the conversation or not. If you were alone, debriefing with your officer helps you capture the details of the meeting and helps your officer stay current on the state of the process. If you were together, sharing your observations will help you identify nuances that only one of you saw or compare your interpretations of information the donor shared. Ask yourself:

- What did I hear?

- What did I see?

- What does that suggest?

- What does the donor expect next?

The answers you provide help determine your follow-up strategy from this visit and help shape your strategy for the next. The last question is particularly important. If you promised to send information or follow up in some way, be sure you do it. Ask your assistant or your development officer to help you keep this top of mind so that it gets done, and soon. If you do not follow up reliably, you will raise questions in your prospects' minds about whether you would be similarly unreliable in administering their gifts.

Creative Interrogation

There are no magical questions that will guarantee you the information you need to prepare your solicitation. As you begin working with donors, ask your development officer for suggestions. Most of us have a group of questions we find to be particularly successful in establishing a bond with a donor and getting the donor to open up and share information. Over time, you will develop your own comfort questions as well.

Ask leading questions because simple yes-or-no questions do not garner much information. Phrase your questions in a way that encourages an expansive answer. Rather than, "Did you take any classes with Professor Smith?" ask, "Who were some of your favorite faculty members?" Listen carefully to answers and ask follow-up questions before moving on to another topic.

Hearing the Donor's Story

A technique that has worked well for me is to ask questions to which I think I already know the answer. For example, my biographical research on the prospect may have told me that her first few jobs after graduation were in a different field from the one in which she currently works. I would then ask, "Have you always been in the [blank] field?" She will then tell me the fact I know, which is that she started out in a different field. Then she will probably go on to tell me why she changed fields, how she got her first job in the new field, or why she likes it better. Her reply will likely prompt follow-up questions I can ask as well. This exchange will give me insight into her decision-making process and what she values about her professional life, and possibly other useful information.

Your development officer has probably learned important information about the prospect in earlier encounters. That provides an opportunity for him or her to say, "I know the dean would love to hear your story about [blank]." The donor may add nuance when telling you the story or may present it slightly differently from how your officer heard it. You and your officer can compare notes later and probably flesh out your understanding of the donor.

Here are some sample questions to consider:

Sample Questions About the Donor's Relationship with the Institution

• Tell me about your time at U of X.

• Whom did you study with?

• Which of your fellow students are you still in contact with?

• Did others in your family attend X College?

• What do you think of the changes in the campus since you were a student?

• What [student organizations, peer groups] have you stayed involved with?

Sample Questions About the Person

• How did you make your way to [this job, this city]?

• How did you start collecting [art, cars]?

• Did you have any time for a vacation this summer?

• What are your plans for the holidays?

• How did you meet your [spouse/partner]?

Sample Questions About the Donor's Philanthropy

• I saw that you [got an award from, joined the board of, attended the gala at] . . .

• How did you get involved with that organization?

Throughout this conversation, keep your antennae finely tuned. If you see the prospect's eyes light up or the body language open up, go further with that topic. As the conversation progresses, begin to offer bits and pieces of information about your program. Recent happenings and new information are natural ways to bring your program into a conversation without appearing to be making a presentation. If the donor seems to respond well to something you share, go a little further. But remember that you will have many other opportunities to talk with this person. You do not have to share everything in this conversation. Just as with your initial meeting, it is good to keep a few things unsaid to provide an obvious opportunity for follow-up.

Throughout cultivation, watch for a spark; then fan the flame.

Cultivation Techniques

Cultivation is more than just visits and meals. The more varied your encounters with a donor, the more varied the information you will exchange, and the more multifaceted your relationship will become. The techniques you use will depend mainly on the prospect's location and personal circumstances. If the donor lives far from campus, you will have to implement the majority of the cultivation phase by going to his or her area. The same will apply if the donor has limited mobility.

Where possible, it is good to have a number of your in-person cultivation encounters occur on campus. In addition to the usual meetings, you can use campus activities as cultivation steps:

- If your prospect is on one of your volunteer committees, be sure to find some dedicated time with the donor in the context of the meeting activities.

- Ask a prospect to attend an athletic or cultural event on the campus as your guest.

- Invite the donor to attend a student event, such as a business plan competition or a research presentation day.

- Alert the prospect that a special guest will be speaking at your program, and offer to introduce the donor to the speaker before or after the presentation.

Between in-person encounters, keep in touch with your prospect by sharing information and through thoughtful gestures:

- Forward a link to a news article on a topic you know is interesting to the donor.

- Personalize a mass mailing, such as your alumni magazine, by sending an advance copy with a note asking for the prospect's thoughts about a particular article.

- Send a birthday card with a handwritten note.

- Start an e-mail conversation about the donor's area of interest by sharing a piece of news.

Solicitation as Cultivation

Many development professionals believe that it is a mistake to ask for an annual gift while in the cultivation phase for a major gift. Their concern is that the lower ask may suggest to the donor that you do not expect a larger gift or that the donor will say, "But I already gave," when the larger ask occurs.

Others believe that solicitations for annual gifts can be woven into the cultivation strategy. They view the annual fund solicitation as establishing a solicitation rapport between the solicitor and the donor and giving the solicitor an opportunity to show the donor a wide range of giving opportunities and needs. Since cultivation can take months or years, annual fund solicitations can be a component in deepening and strengthening the relationship in advance of a major gift solicitation. They address their colleagues' concerns about donor confusion by noting that someone who can afford to give a major gift will know the difference between $25,000 and $2,500, and will not be surprised by an additional, larger solicitation.

There is no one right way to settle this issue. You should ascertain the philosophy of your campus's development leadership and discuss this with your own development officer.

Clear Communication About Types of Gifts

If you do choose to solicit your major gift prospects for annual gifts, be clear about what you are asking the donor to support. You might say, "I hope over time we'll have an opportunity to discuss a major commitment to the program. In the meantime, we've benefited greatly from your annual support, and I'd like to ask you to continue that this year." Donors with significant capacity are solicited frequently by many organizations. It is unlikely that you will do any harm to the relationship by putting this request forward.

Moving from Cultivation to Solicitation

The cultivation phase varies from donor to donor and can take anywhere from a few weeks to many months. How do we know when the relationship has progressed to the point where we can move from the cultivation stage into the solicitation stage?

A simple test is to revisit the question, "Am I going to ask for a gift today?" If you cannot identify a legitimate reason not to ask in your next visit, then it is time to move on. (If your answer is, "No, because I'm scared," then hang on. The next chapter addresses that.)

Sometimes the donor makes it obvious that he or she is ready for the solicitation. Any version of, "What can I do to help?" is a clear signal of this intent. If a donor asks that question and you do not yet have a clear sense of what you would like to ask for, reply, "I'd like to count on you for a major commitment to our program. As I prepare a proposal for you to consider, what would you like it to include?" This will give you the most specific information you could possibly have in crafting your solicitation. It should also give you a significant incentive to figure out your ask and make it soon.

Sometimes you will sense that the time may be right, but you would like to be more confident of the donor's readiness before presenting a solicitation. In that case, you can use a *soft ask* to confirm your assessment and alert the donor that you feel it is time to discuss a gift.

A *hard ask* is a request that includes specifics such as a dollar amount, a designation, timing, and perhaps other logistical components—for example, "Will you support our scholarship initiative by giving $25,000 over the next five years to endow a scholarship for literature majors?" It also encourages the donor to make a definitive decision, whether today or after a contemplation period, about a commitment.

A soft ask does not include these specifics. Rather, it is a request for information or confirmation regarding solicitation readiness. You can think of it as a pre-ask, or asking permission to ask. A soft ask does not seek a firm yes or no about the gift itself. Rather it asks for a yes or no regarding the process's moving forward—for example:

"The next time we get together, could we talk about your campaign gift?"

"How would you feel about my bringing you some funding ideas to consider?"

"At what point during our get-togethers would you like to discuss your gift to your program?"

"Have you thought about what role you would like to play in our project?"

Each of these queries gives the donor the opportunity to tell you whether it is time. If it is not, this approach gives the donor a graceful way to say so without having to decline a direct solicitation. By this time, you and the donor have developed a friendly relationship. The donor probably would feel uncomfortable about disappointing you by declining a solicitation. It is much easier for a donor who is not yet ready for a solicitation to say, "Not right now," or, "Maybe later," than to say, "No, I won't give."

If you have presented a soft ask and your donor has not responded favorably, listen carefully because your donor is telling you what your continued cultivation strategy should be. Whether it is more time or more information or any other concern, you must meet the donor's needs before you can be assured of success in the solicitation.

But if the donor is receptive and indicates that he or she is ready to talk, you can move on to the solicitation with confidence.

10

Solicitation

By the time you are ready to ask for a major gift, your relation-ship with the prospective donor is deep and engaged. You have become partners with a common interest in the success of your program. Making a gift provides the donor with a tangible way to move toward your shared goals.

New academic administrators sometimes express anxiety over the actual act of solicitation. They worry that the interaction will involve begging or trying to persuade the potential donor to under-take an unpleasant task. If you feel this hesitation, spend some time with donors who have already made their gifts. Ask them how the act of giving made them feel. The joy they express, the warmth, the enthusiasm, and the sense of fulfillment should resolve any concern you have about what you would be putting your donors through by helping them make a gift.

Even with this insight, you may still feel uncomfortable directly asking for money. That is okay. You can be an effective member of a solicitation team without being the one who asks for the gift. Your fundraiser has the skills and experience to ask with confi-dence and should accompany you on solicitation calls regardless of which of you will be articulating the ask. You can set the stage and inspire the donor, and your fundraiser can ask. Donors will feel they are giving to you because you embody the program in their minds. They may not even notice that you were not the one who actually delivered the solicitation.

There are no magical words or techniques that will guarantee success in a solicitation. But there is one core requirement without which a major solicitation is sure to fail: an absolute alignment of values and goals between the potential donor and the institution.

Donors do not give merely because our programs need and deserve support. They give because of their own desires, passions, and aspirations. If our worthiness were the only requirement, no deserving organization would lack for funds. Donors turn their interest into investment when it feels right to them to do so. That rarely happens without a complete synchronization between donor and recipient.

To ensure that our solicitation is aligned properly, we must know a number of things about the donor's motivations:

- What does this person value?

- What is she trying to accomplish?

- What is really important to him?

- What does she want her legacy to be?

- What impact does he want to have?

- Where do our programs and priorities coincide with
  the prospect's values, desires, and aspirations?

If you cannot answer these questions with certainty, it is not yet time to solicit. Continue to cultivate the relationship, with your strategy being to gain the additional information you need to ensure this absolute alignment.

Components of an Ask

You and your development officer should collaboratively develop a strategy for the ask that has four key factors: how much, for what, when, and why.

How Much

Determining the appropriate dollar amount for the ask may be the most difficult component of preparing for a solicitation. In the best-case scenario, your cultivation conversations will have included a soft ask that has prompted the donor to tell you the range of giving he or she is considering. You may also have the benefit of having discussed an opportunity with the donor where a specific giving level is commonly known among your constituency, such as establishing an endowment or funding a space in a building project.

If a figure has never come up in discussion, you and your officer must attempt to identify an ask level that will be both possible for and attractive to the donor. Your officer will have acquired as much information about wealth indicators as your prospect researchers can find. This information may paint a broad picture, but it will not give you a precise target. Wealthy people have many methods for shielding their net worth from curious seekers. And even when you have a good sense of the prospect's assets, you usually cannot ascertain how liquid those assets are. For example, an entrepreneur with a $100 million stake in a company cannot give that $100 million away. Some of it may be in salable securities, but it is likely that a great deal of it is leveraged within the business or constrained against liquidation.

To the financial information you attain, add the factor of prior giving behavior. If the target ask you are planning is considerably more than the donor has ever given before, to your institution or any other that you know of, the solicitation process may be complex. It may require more negotiation regarding the technicalities of fulfilling the commitment.

If you are not confident that you have determined an amount to solicit, be prepared to offer the donor a range of opportunities within his or her area of interest. For example, show the donor several options for creating endowments to support faculty:

- $5 million for a distinguished chair

- $2 million for a chair

- $1 million for a professorship

- $500,000 for a research fellowship

- $100,000 for a curriculum development fund

- $50,000 for a faculty research travel prize

As you discuss these options, the donor will likely indicate the level at which he or she is prepared to commit. The level may be higher than you expected. If it is lower, you can discuss possibilities for increasing the endowment to higher levels with future gifts, and you will have raised the donor's sights regarding what larger gifts can accomplish.

For What

During the cultivation process, you will have identified the donor's particular area of interest. Now that it is time to solicit, use the information you have gained to suggest a specific designation. Continuing the faculty example, you would tailor the options to reflect a department or program or even a general field of study in which the donor has expressed interest.

When

On what time line will you ask the donor to complete the gift? Remember that our desired timing for projects may not coincide with the donor's preferred time line for funding an opportunity. Although we can share timing issues such as campaign end dates or project targets, these are not generally the deciding factors in donors' financial decisions. The exception will be when external timing issues have a significant impact on the overall project. For example, a construction schedule that requires decisions on building configurations or a faculty recruitment opportunity that must be addressed quickly can prompt the donor to commit quickly.

For outright gifts, the timing questions are generally limited to whether the gift will be made in a single payment or whether it will be spread across several pledge payments. Deferred gifts can be significantly more complex. In these cases, you may not have access to the corpus of the gift for some time, possibly even beyond the donor's lifetime. If you are discussing a project that will be implemented sooner, you may have to explore creative funding mechanisms to meet both your and the donor's goals.

Why

What does this opportunity offer the donor, and what impact will the gift have on the institution? This is the most important component of the request. It is the expression of the confluence of your goals and the donor's goals. It is a simple, powerful statement that connects what the donor wants with what your program needs—for example, "Your dream of helping the children of immigrants achieve a college education can be brought to life by our new scholarship program." If you have asked the right questions and listened carefully to the answers during the cultivation process, your donor will respond, "Yes, I want to make that happen."

The Solicitation Team

Major asks are best delivered by a team, each of whose members plays a defined role in the conversation. You and your development officer are the foundation of the team, and often only the two of you will be needed. To determine whether you should add other members to the team, ask these questions:

- Who should be present to create the best experience for the potential donor?

- Whom is the prospect most likely to say yes to?

- Who is the institution's best representative of the area you are asking the donor to support?

You can engage others in your solicitation in a variety of ways. There may be someone close to the prospect who will be influential in the prospect's decision, such as a volunteer peer or the president of the university. That person should be present for the actual ask. Your program representatives, however, may not need to be present for that part of the meeting.

For example, you and your development officer take the prospect to a faculty member's lab. The prospect interacts with the faculty member and the graduate students. They discuss the work they are doing and the limitations placed on them by the outdated laboratory facilities. You and the development officer then take the prospect back to your office, where you ask for a gift for lab renovation. This gives the prospect a direct view of the impact a gift would have and enables you to engage other members of your community in inspiring the donor without having to deliver a solicitation themselves.

Whether the team consists only of you and your development officer or other parties are involved, it is critical to plan in advance who will present what information and who will answer what questions. This ensures that the conversation will flow naturally, with each of you participating in the ways that you are most comfortable. A common division of roles is to have you present information and field questions about the program, while the development officer presents information and answers questions regarding the logistics and technicalities of giving. Knowing that you need not be deeply conversant on the technicalities of giving allows you to relax and focus on what you know best, certain that your development partner can provide expert content in those other areas. A peer volunteer can provide an endorsement of the project, an example of his or her own giving, or information regarding the volunteer group's participation in the project.

The team should gather to rehearse well before the actual meeting. Ask other development colleagues to join you at this rehearsal to give you feedback and help you prepare. During the rehearsal, practice how you will word the ask, and discuss how you will handle questions you anticipate the donor may raise. You may find that when you initially articulate a message, it is not as clear or effective as you imagined it would be. This rehearsal gives you an opportunity to try various approaches and fine-tune your content so that it comes naturally when it is time to deliver it to the donor.

Preparing for the Solicitation Meeting

Now that you have determined what the ask will contain, you or your development officer should contact the prospect to set up a meeting. During this exchange, you should clearly communicate that you would like to discuss the donor's giving during this upcoming meeting. It is important for the donor to be ready to have this conversation. Agreeing on the nature of it in advance gives the donor time to address any issues that he or she needs to resolve before the meeting. For instance, the donor may have advisers such as financial planners or trust attorneys to consult or may want to include a partner or other family in the discussion. Most important, if the donor is not ready to discuss a gift, you will learn this now, saving both you and the donor from an awkward encounter.

Choose a location for the meeting that will be conducive to the solicitation conversation. It should be a venue with relative privacy because the donor may not wish to discuss personal financial information if others can overhear. An on-campus location is ideal if it is convenient for the donor to get to you. If you are going to the donor's location, ask whether the home or office would be preferable to the donor. Couples often make the giving decisions jointly, which may suggest a home visit rather than a visit to either party's office.

If you are meeting for a meal, choose a restaurant with widely spaced tables and good acoustics. The solicitation will not go smoothly if you and the prospect cannot hear each other over the din of other diners.

Review your solicitation plan to create an agenda for the conversation. Based on the amount of time you think you will have, decide what to cover and when to move to the solicitation. A meeting in the donor's office is usually much shorter than a dinner meeting. In the former case, you might move directly from catching up into the solicitation. In the latter, there would be time to discuss several topics before presenting the ask.

This agenda should be a mental one, not a written one. Review it with your development partner until you both have it fully committed to memory. You want this conversation to be as natural and comfortable as possible, and a written agenda adds a level of formality that can be an impediment.

Prepare any materials you are using. You should take only those that will move the conversation forward. Campaign case statements and program brochures are good educational tools, but they will accomplish nothing in a solicitation meeting. An example of appropriate materials would be renderings of a proposed renovation or new facility for which you are seeking the donor's support. You can use these during the conversation to show the donor what the space will be like and where his or her funded area will be.

Should I Take a Written Proposal?

Many of my development colleagues would disagree, but I recommend against taking a written proposal to the solicitation meeting. This is intended to be a conversation. You do not need a written document to get the conversation going, and if your intention is to leave the proposal for the donor to review after your meeting, consider that you and the donor may learn things from each other that you did not previously know. If you have already prepared the follow-up document, you are implying to the donor that you already know the outcome of the conversation. Finally, offering to draw up a formal proposal is an excellent next step from this meeting. It allows you and your development officer to fully incorporate the content of the meeting. And a follow-up document creates a natural reason for you and the donor to be in touch soon.

Finally, be sure that you and your team know how to get to the meeting location and how long it will take. Include extra time for travel. Arriving late and starting the meeting with flustered apologies is uncomfortable for you and the donor.

Conducting the Meeting

Before you leave for the meeting, review your mental agenda one last time and ask yourself if you are truly ready. It is common to be nervous. Your development officer will understand and can help you feel more comfortable. If you have changed your mind and no longer feel confident about making the ask yourself, say so now. Your development officer can easily take over that part of the conversation, but only if he or she knows that is what you want.

Once you have exchanged pleasantries and caught up on recent happenings with the donor, turn the conversation to the solicitation. Acknowledge the reason for the visit, and deliver the ask you have rehearsed. Be straightforward and clear. Do not try to cushion the ask or surround it in a flowery context. The donor knows what this conversation is about. The simpler your approach is, the sooner you and the donor can move into a discussion.

When you (or your development partner) have articulated the request, stop talking. Give the donor time to process what you have said. Even if the pause seems to stretch for hours, master your impulse to fill the silence. The initial response from the donor sets the tone for the rest of the conversation. You must remain quiet and listen carefully to determine how to proceed.

Sometimes the response is an immediate and happy yes, in which case you can move directly into a discussion of the logistics of making the gift. More often the donor has questions or thoughts, and a discussion ensues. Let the donor lead this part of the conversation. Trying to anticipate what the donor is thinking may only lead you to answer questions he or she was not planning to ask or address concerns the donor does not have.

During this phase of the conversation, it may not yet be obvious whether the donor is going to commit to the gift. Be careful not to let that uncertainty overwhelm your good judgment. Do not offer enticements or make promises you will not be able to keep. Listen to the donor, respond candidly and honestly, and allow the donor's thought process to play out.

Solicitations of large gifts often take multiple conversations. Do not be concerned if the donor appears to need more time before deciding. If it is ultimately not clear whether the donor wants to make a decision or prefers to continue on to another meeting, ask a question like, "How would you like to proceed?" This will generally evoke a clear statement from the donor regarding what should happen next.

As the conversation moves to a conclusion, you or your development officer should verbalize the next steps. These may include gathering more information or preparing a written proposal. If the donor has not yet made a firm decision, one of you should say, "Could we put these ideas in writing and send them to you for you to review?" Sending a written follow-up then sets the stage for you or your development officer to make a subsequent phone call to see if the prospect has questions about the written proposal. This keeps the momentum of the conversation in your hands and lowers the risk that the process will falter because the donor gets busy and forgets to take the next step.

Close the meeting with a genuine thank-you. Even if the donor has not given, he or she has at least given you time and consideration.

After the Meeting

Immediately after the meeting, have a debriefing session with your development partner and any others who were at the meeting. Your varied perspectives and observations will combine to create a fully faceted report on the discussion. Review who is responsible for each component of follow-up and the time line for completion.

Then be sure to do everything you have promised to do, as quickly as possible. The donor has left this meeting with a sense of enthusiasm about the possibility of having an impact through giving. Capitalize on that enthusiasm and move into the next conversation before it wanes.

Once the Gift Has Been Secured

Everything about a gift commitment should be documented in writing. Your university's development office has standard practices for this documentation. Let your development partner guide this process. There are many components of gift, pledge, and endowment agreements that have legal and tax ramifications. If you attempt to create your own documentation, you may inadvertently create undesired consequences for the university or the donor.

You should discuss with the donor how news of the gift will be shared and what level of public recognition will be associated with the gift. Keep the news of this gift strictly confidential until all of the details have been determined and the paperwork has been signed. Although it is uncommon, sometimes donors change their minds during the process of formalizing the gift. You will avoid awkwardness all around if you have not shared the news beyond those who need to know in order to help with the documentation.

If the Donor Says No

There are many variations of no in a major gift solicitation conversation. When you set up the meeting, you conveyed to the donor that you were planning on discussing a gift when you got together. Donors who have no interest in giving will not accept such a meeting. Thus, it is unlikely that any version of no during this conversation is a complete refusal. This no is probably an indication that something about the gift you proposed is not yet in sync with what the donor would like to do. Most donors will immediately move from "no" to "because." This is the most important time to listen. While you may be feeling discouraged or disappointed that the solicitation is not going as planned, you need to pay close attention to every nuance of the donor's explanation for declining. It is likely that you and your development officer can address the concerns that are preventing the donor from committing—but only if you listen carefully to fully understand what they are.

You may be able to address the donor's objections on the spot. If the dollar amount or the timing of the gift you have proposed does not work for the donor, you and your development officer can offer alternatives that may resolve the concerns immediately. In the case of more complex objections, you may not be able to address the situation immediately. Be sure that you understand what the donor needs to feel comfortable making the gift, and then suggest meeting again after you have had an opportunity to investigate possible resolutions.

Do not offer to resolve something over which you do not have either control or authority. For example, the donor may believe that the university's investment strategy is too conservative, and the payout from endowed funds is too low. Unless you have unilateral authority over your university's investment policies, do not offer to change anything about these practices. Instead, you might offer to ask your chief financial officer to meet with the donor to discuss the rationale behind the policies. Or your development officer might offer to discuss options for externally held trusts, assuming your university accepts these. That type of giving vehicle would allow the donor to fund the program year by year while retaining more control over investment strategies.

Throughout the discussion that ensues after the no, show the donor the same respect you would have shown if the answer had been yes. If the concerns have not been resolved during this conversation, you should still articulate next steps and timing. As we have referenced repeatedly, this is a long-term relationship. You would not end a personal friendship over one denied request; neither should you convey in any way that this relationship is contingent on this gift.

Sample Responses to Common Objections

There are a few concerns that donors raise frequently enough that you should be prepared to address them. The sample language here is intended to serve as a starting point for a conversation between you and your development officer. You can also discuss recurring objections that are idiosyncratic to your institution. Rehearsing your responses with your officer will increase your comfort when you face these obstacles in actual solicitations.

"I could never give that much."

Development officers learn never to assume that individuals who have the capacity to make major gifts also have a sophisticated understanding of how this type of giving works. This objection sometimes means that the donor cannot give that much right now or all at one time. In that case, sharing information about multiyear pledges may resolve the objection immediately.

If you have indeed overestimated the donor's capacity, tread carefully. Traditional fundraising lore holds that it is a compliment to donors to ask for too much, because it implies that they seem to be people of greater wealth. On the contrary, many fundraisers can attest that it merely embarrasses donors to have to admit that they do not have sufficient wealth to help a cause they love at the level you have asked.

This is a good time to discuss the stepped levels recommended earlier in this chapter. Sharing lower-level giving opportunities within the same program gives the donor the possibility of saying yes at a more comfortable dollar amount.

"I can't give a big gift until I have taken care of my family."

This is a common concern for donors who have just moved into their prime giving years. Their wealth peaks at a time when they are assessing how to care for aging parents or confronting the possibility that their adult children may not be independent after all. Let your development officer introduce the idea of planned giving. Your university development program should have officers who are highly trained in the wide array of giving options that offer donors the ability to cover their, and their family's, financial needs while also benefiting the university now and in the future.

"There are other organizations that need my money much more than the university does."

A number of factors lead the public to believe that all universities are wealthy. The sheer size of our operations, public discourse around large endowments and high tuition, and our own efforts to share our accomplishments can create the impression that we have all we need. Meanwhile, the number of small, struggling nonprofit organizations grows. Donors can feel conflicted about apportioning their philanthropic dollars, wanting to be sure that they are creating the largest impact possible with their own finite resources.

Do not attempt to make the case that the university is as needy as other organizations the donor supports. All of these needs are legitimate, and trying to discount the other organizations' importance will make you seem insensitive and may alienate the donor. Rather, acknowledge and praise the generosity of the donor across an array of causes. Convey to the donor your hope that your program will have a place in that array.

Then share the effect this gift will have on individuals. Tell the story of a student or faculty member who will directly benefit from support of this program. Turning the conversation away from need and toward impact creates an appropriate comparison point for the donor to consider.

11

Stewardship

Our relationships with donors after they have made their gifts are just as complex and productive as during the cultivation and solicitation processes. We have legal and moral obligations to steward the resources with which donors have entrusted us. Simultaneously, we are stewarding our institutional relationships with our supporters.

By giving us major gifts, donors place their faith in our capacity to effect the change they are funding. They rely on our trustworthiness to care for their investment and use it properly. For donors who have not yet given their ultimate lifetime gift, the way we handle their current gifts is an important factor in their consideration of future gifts.

Giving is a form of investing. Although the returns are obviously quite different from the returns on personal financial investments, our donors want many of the same things from our institutions that they want from the financial institutions in which they have entrusted their personal funds. Consider your own personal investments. Consider what you expect from the banks or investment firms that are holding your resources:

- *Security.* Your investment will be kept safe and protected.

- *Reliability.* Your investment will be tended in the ways you expected when you chose that institution.

- *Sound strategies.* You want to be confident that this firm knows what it is doing and thus will not expose you to unnecessary risk.

- *Accurate information.* You want to know exactly what happens with your money.

- *Timely and thorough reporting.* You expect to hear about activity on a regular basis, without having to seek out the information yourself.

- *Clear communication.* Representatives of the financial institution should be available to you and should be willing and able to answer any questions you have about your funds.

All of these factors are also part of donors' expectations from us as we implement the investments they have made through their giving. If we do not meet these expectations, dissatisfied donors may stop giving or move their gifts elsewhere. They will also tell their friends and associates about the experiences they have with our programs, good or bad. Thus, every component of our stewardship program has potentially widespread ramifications.

As you define your overall stewardship program, also define who is responsible for implementing each component of the plan. Some of these gifts will be stewarded for decades, and it is important that the process not dissipate during staff transitions. In the context of these assignments, identify the roles that are important for you to play. Keep in mind that your presence signifies stature and importance to donors. While you can steward the entire community in a general way, focus your personalized stewardship activities on the highest tier of donors.

The Stewardship Cycle

The cycle of stewardship begins with acknowledgment of the gift, moves through recognition of the donor, and then settles into an indeterminate period of implementing the gift and enjoying its impact. The expansiveness and intensity of each of these stages vary from donor to donor, primarily based on the size of the gift.

Acknowledgment

The way in which you document and acknowledge a gift is the first indication you give donors of how well you will handle the investment they have made in your program. Acknowledgments must be prompt, thorough, accurate, and meaningful. This begins with a formal confirmation to the donor of the recording of a pledge or the transfer of funds. This should state the dollar amount, the date of the commitment, and the designation for which it will be used. The central development office generally handles these first-line acknowledgments because it has the most current information on tax codes and other legalities involved in gift receipting.

Once the confirmation has been provided, the appropriate representatives of the university should thank the donor. Opinions vary regarding how many thank-yous are appropriate. Some development professionals believe that donors are overwhelmed when they get several thank-you letters, and the messages lose their impact. Others feel that an outpouring of gratitude makes donors feel special and appreciated. Determine what approach your university takes, and orient your thank-you messages within it.

Most campus-level programs take a tiered approach to the level of thanks provided to the donor. Those who have made relatively small gifts may receive a preprinted thank-you card with the formal receipt. Those giving somewhat larger gifts, perhaps at the high end of annual giving, may receive a preprinted note, but it is sent separately from the receipt and is hand-signed with a personalized message. At higher gift amounts still, the acknowledgment is in the form of a letter signed by a university official; this may be the vice president for development, a senior academic administrator (possibly you), or the president.

Some universities have policies defining at what gift level presidential thanks are sent and how the timing of presidential thanks affects the timing of thank-yous from other university representatives. You may be asked to wait until the presidential acknowledgment has been sent before you send your own.

Within your college, you should establish your own tiered acknowledgment system. Your thresholds for escalating acknowledgments may differ from those at the campus level, particularly if you are a unit that receives most of its gifts as outright gifts to the annual fund.

While the impulse to thank every donor deeply and effusively is a generous one, it is important to moderate your thanks at the lowest levels. As donors give increasingly larger gifts over time, they should receive increasingly significant acknowledgment of those gifts. If you lavish all available enthusiasm on a $25 donor, what is the reward for a donor who gives $25,000?

One of the simplest and most effective forms of acknowledgment is a phone call to thank the donor. You and your development staff should identify a giving level above which every donor gets a thank-you call. If your program is small, this may even be every donor. Making these calls yourself is a high-impact, low-time-commitment way of increasing your presence with donors. The calls are brief, and in many cases result in messages left on answering machines. The basic message is:

> Hello, Dr. Smith. This is Dean Johnson calling from the College of Arts and Sciences at State University. I've just learned that your gift to the annual fund has arrived, and I'm calling to say thank-you. We couldn't achieve our goals without the support of donors like you. Thank you for having faith in us and in our students. I'm sorry to have missed you, but I can be reached at (555) 555-5555 if you'd like to be in touch.

This simple, thirty-second message will likely make the day of the donor you call. And when you do connect with someone, the resulting conversation is practically guaranteed to put a smile on both of your faces.

Recognition

Some donors prefer not to attract the spotlight with their giving, some even going so far as to require that their gifts remain anonymous. With very large gifts, the likelihood of donors' wishing to have some level of public recognition rises. They may be making the gift to honor someone who is important to them, and they want to draw attention to the honoree. They may hope to set an example for their peers and spur additional giving. And some just like the attention.

As with acknowledgments, recognition of gifts should be calibrated to the size and impact of the gift. It is likely that your campus has standards regarding the level of visibility afforded to gifts at various levels. Consistent campuswide compliance with these standards must be maintained so that donors do not feel they can get more visible recognition from some colleges than from others.

The precise nature of recognition should be negotiated during the gift discussions, especially for large gifts. You do not want to discover after the fact that the donor wants a level of recognition that you cannot provide. Before you make any promises during these discussions, be sure that what you are offering is acceptable within the campus's policies. This is particularly important if you are planning to offer to name a space or post a plaque or other permanent signage. Most campuses have requirements regarding size, graphic style, and placement. There may also be an approval process you must go through before confirming the naming. As a side note, when there is to be signage in recognition of a gift, expect to pay for that out of your own budget. Few universities have a central budget for this, and it is unseemly to ask the donor to pay for it.

Donors at more modest gift levels may be recognized within a group context, perhaps in the form of a donor honor roll, a listing in your program's publication, a donor wall, or some other physical representation showing all who have contributed to a particular fund or project. Keep in mind that recognition vehicles have costs, both direct and indirect. An honor roll may be a good way to show your donors the community in which they belong, and it may spur donors to give again to ensure being listed the following year. In addition to the positive effects, consider the costs associated with design, printing, and mailing, along with the significant quantity of staff time that is required to prepare a complete and completely accurate honor roll. Based on your own program's culture and circumstances, decide whether the benefits justify the costs.

Giving societies are another vehicle for providing group recognition. More information on giving societies can be found in Chapter Fourteen.

Long-Term Management

For the life of the gift, which will be forever if the gift is to endowment, your university has a responsibility to ensure that the gift is used according to the agreement between the university and the donor. A signed gift agreement is a contract, and if you violate it, you face the possibility that the donor will seek recourse. There is no good outcome when an angry, disillusioned donor takes action against the recipient organization, whether in the courts or in the media. Honoring donor intent is the most important component of the ongoing management phase of stewardship.

Your business manager and your development officer should conduct regular reviews of all of your college's gift funds to ensure that proper documentation is in place regarding the use of the funds and that expenditures from the funds are consistent with the donor's intent. An important component of this review is determining whether all available gift funds are being spent. Older funds may have escaped notice during staff turnover and may be

sitting fallow. This should be rectified immediately, out of obliga-
tion to the original donor. It is also important not to send a signal
to potential donors that you do not need the funds you have, much
less the ones they may give. Some universities ask their internal
audit function to review randomly selected accounts to help reassure donors that the university is firmly committed to using gifts
appropriately.

The central development office probably has a process for communicating with endowment donors on an annual basis regarding
the performance and the beneficiaries of the funds they have established. The central office can provide the financial information,
but you must provide the information regarding impact. A report
from the faculty member who holds an endowed chair or a thank-
you note from a student who has received a scholarship is generally
much more meaningful to a donor than the financial report on the
endowed fund.

You can supplement this annual report with occasional infor-
mal reports. Send an e-mail when the faculty member wins an
award or the student receives an honor. Share progress on a donor-
funded renovation project or student activity. This shows donors
that your program cares about their satisfaction, and it reminds
them of the impact their gift is having. Your development officer
can provide you with prompts for these communications.

Though it occurs infrequently, you should be prepared for the
possibility that something will go wrong with a gift during this
long-term management: the holder of an endowed chair may be
involved in a scandal, the student receiving a scholarship may
flunk out, or the renovated space may be discovered to have toxic
mold. Whatever the negative development, be sure that any donors
associated with the situation hear about it from you first. While
maintaining an appropriate level of professional confidentiality,
contact the donors to alert them that they may hear news of this.
Assure them that you are doing everything within your power to
resolve the situation. Then keep the donors appropriately informed

as events unfold. The donors may be unhappy about what has happened, but they will appreciate the care you have shown in communicating with them.

Occasionally a university is no longer able to honor a donor's previously established intent. This generally happens with long-established endowed funds that have designation criteria that are no longer appropriate, for example, faculty chairs in programs that have been discontinued and scholarships with restrictions that can no longer be found in your student body. Many gift agreements will have language on alternate use that specifies how the gift should be used if the original intent can no longer be honored. If you face such a situation, do everything you can to find the original donor or the donor's heirs. Conferring with them to determine a use that is consistent with the donor's original wishes is the best outcome for all involved. If you make these decisions without such consultation and the donor or family discover the change after the fact, you will likely face significant dissatisfaction and possible legal ramifications. Your development office can advise you on all the necessary steps to document whatever decisions are made.

Common Stewardship Techniques

Many of the techniques for cultivation reviewed in Chapter Nine are appropriate during stewardship. The deepening of the relationship and strengthening of the bond between the donor and the institution are goals during this period just as they were during the cultivation period.

The right stewardship activities for your donor constituency should be determined in consultation with your development staff, taking into account the nature and culture of your supporters. Here are some common techniques for you to consider.

Continued Visits

Some donors hesitate to finalize their gift because they fear they will no longer have the close contact with you and your staff that they have come to enjoy. You may not need to visit donors who are in long-term stewardship as often as you visit those with whom you are discussing upcoming gifts. But keep them on your visit list, and get together from time to time.

Events

Donor recognition events are a good experience for both the donors who are being recognized and the guests who are awed by their generosity. Keep in mind that the IRS limits the deductibility of contributions when goods or services have been received in exchange for the gift. If you present an event as a specific benefit for donors in exchange for their gifts of a particular level, you will probably have to alter their gift receipts accordingly. It is better not to link events to gifts during the solicitation process, but rather to hold them for the good of the community, including a variety of guests.

Communication

Consider whether your regular communication pieces for your entire constituency can be customized for donors. Perhaps they can receive an alumni magazine or e-newsletter earlier than the general constituency or receive a personalized note with their copy. Be sure to convey that this is happening because of their special status as donors to your program.

Mementos

This is a hotly debated issue among development officers. Some love to have small items to share with donors during visits. Others feel that their donors have all the paperweights and T-shirts they could possibly need and do not want their gifts spent on creating trinkets to be given back to them. If you are considering producing mementos for your donors, confer with a few of your closest donor friends to determine whether this is a good idea and, if it is, what type of memento will be most effective. As with events, be careful of IRS regulations regarding the value of gifts you give donors.

Special Access

You can communicate how much you value donors by including them in special opportunities at your college. Examples are a private coffee with a noted speaker after a public lecture, or a discussion with students and faculty after a performance. These activities deepen the donors' connections to your program without significant expense to you.

Stewardship to Cultivation

As we saw in Chapter Six, the process of stewarding a relationship after a gift can serve as a transition into cultivation for a subsequent gift. Donors usually indicate when a major gift is the last one they intend to make. If they have not indicated that they have finished their lifetime giving, use your stewardship relationship to explore future giving possibilities. There is no set period you should expect to wait between gifts. Some donors are ready to give again quickly, and others space their gifts over many years.

Assessing the possibility of another solicitation should be a subtle, gradual process and should not be the focus of the relationship until well after the initial gift has been made and recognized. As your contact with the donor continues, assess what you learn just as you did during the cultivation process. The donor may show interest in giving more to the original area of support or may begin to express enthusiasm for another area of your program. Confer with your development officer about the signs you see. Work together to develop a new cultivation and solicitation strategy when the donor is receptive.

Case Study

Engaging High-Profile Alumni

Connie Contributor is a corporate litigator who received her law degree from Sample University. She is frequently associated with high-profile cases that last for several years and result in victories for Connie's clients in the tens of millions of dollars. She has become a media celebrity due to her charisma and quick wit. She appears frequently on national television news programs and was recently profiled in a national news magazine as representing the new generation of superstars.

Connie had arrived at the law school as a student with high potential but low means. She was the first in her family to attend college and had worked her way through her undergraduate education. She had received numerous scholarships, but still had incurred a significant loan debt. She blazed through law school, winning every award and honor. Yet she had had little contact with the law school since her graduation. She lived in another city, had never attended alumni events on campus or in her home city, and had never responded to any fundraising appeals. The law alumni magazine staff contacted her office with a request for an interview, but she did not return the call.

When a long-sitting dean retired, a new dean was recruited from the faculty of a top-tier law school. The dean came into his position with an agenda for the college that involved raising its admissions standards, recruiting top faculty, and significantly increasing its fundraising performance. He quickly engaged the current faculty and made progress on his goals.

The college development officer had identified the college's top fifteen donors prior to the dean's arrival. Establishing relationships with these existing supporters was the dean's first development priority. Then he moved on to a more demanding list: twenty-five alumni who had the financial means to be major donors but had not yet made significant commitments to the college. Connie was at the top of this list.

The development officer had tried to connect with Connie through a variety of methods. Phone calls, e-mails, letters, and introductions from other alumni had all proved unsuccessful. The officer hoped that Connie would respond to a direct approach from the dean, despite her disregard for contacts from staff members. At the officer's suggestion, the dean's assistant called Connie's office and told her assistant that the dean was hoping for a quick conversation with one of his most prominent alumni. The dean's assistant gave Connie's assistant her own office number, as well as the dean's direct cell phone number.

That evening, the dean received a call on his cell phone from a number he did not recognize. He answered, and Connie was on the other end of the phone. After introducing herself and exchanging pleasantries, Connie began what the dean later laughingly referred to as an interrogation. She asked him questions about his background, his opinions of the law school, his vision for the future, and his plans. An attorney himself, the dean was not put off by Connie's approach and felt that their conversation was productive. He told her he hoped to meet with her and discuss the college further. She said she would be in touch.

Later that evening, the dean e-mailed Connie at her corporate address. He thanked her for her call and reiterated his interest in meeting with her to continue their discussion.

Several months went by with no contact. The dean had planned a trip to Connie's city, and he e-mailed her to see if she would be available for a visit. She did not reply. Then the development officer noticed a mention in a local newspaper column that Connie would be in the university's city to receive an award from the regional chapter of the American Bar Association. The officer immediately brought this to the dean's attention. He e-mailed Connie to ask if she had time to get together during her visit, but she did not reply.

The dean bought a table at the awards dinner and filled it with law school faculty and students. During the reception before dinner, he approached Connie and introduced himself, saying that it was nice to meet her in person at last. She responded that she knew she owed him responses to his e-mails and didn't want him to think she thought ill of the school. She had been busy and had not made connecting with him a priority. He asked if he could call her office for an appointment, and she agreed.

The following week, the dean's assistant called Connie's assistant and referenced the brief exchange the dean had had with Connie at the reception. Connie's assistant confirmed that Connie had told her to move ahead with scheduling an appointment. Her assistant asked the dean's assistant when the dean would next be in Connie's city. As the development officer had suggested, the dean's assistant replied, "The first time Ms. Contributor is available to see him." They set an appointment for the following week, and the dean's assistant made his travel plans.

The meeting took place in Connie's office. When the dean arrived, he noted that she was surrounded by staff, and that messages and queries were being delivered to her almost constantly. Despite that, he found that she concentrated intently on their conversation. They spoke for twenty minutes before Connie said she had to excuse herself to prepare for a client meeting. As he rose to leave, the dean made an appeal:

> From our brief encounters, I can tell that you and I see eye to eye about the future of the law school. I'm looking for a small number of key advisers to serve as my kitchen cabinet. Can I count you among the membership?

Connie said yes without hesitation.

The dean had secured similar commitments from several other high-profile alumni. Feeling he had reached a critical mass, he called the first meeting of the group. He did not give the group a formal name. Rather, he continued to refer to them as his kitchen cabinet. He set a date and e-mailed the group. To his surprise, Connie replied personally to the e-mail, agreeing to come to campus on the date in question.

The meeting of the group was a success. Their proximity to other alumni of significant accomplishment brought out the best in each of them. The dean posed provocative questions, listened to their ideas, and engaged them in lively debate. The meeting was set for half a day, and after lunch, the group disbanded. On her way to the airport, Connie e-mailed the dean, saying, "I haven't had that much fun in years."

As part of his follow-up communication after the meeting, the dean asked Connie by e-mail if she would come to campus to speak to students. He identified this as part of his strategy to provide students with role models for their careers and to set their sights high regarding their own potential for success. Several days later, Connie's assistant contacted the dean's assistant to set a time for a campus visit.

The dean and his development officer carefully selected a group of students to meet with Connie while she was on campus. They arranged a lunch with the law school's newest faculty, all of whom were rising stars. They packed her visit with activity, and the dean accompanied her every step of the way. The development officer escorted them from venue to venue and attended most of the sessions. By the end of the day, Connie was interacting as comfortably with the development officer as she was with the dean.

As Connie entered her limousine to leave for the airport, she asked the dean and development officer, "Why haven't you asked me for money?"

The dean quickly replied:

> We'd like to. Can we discuss a gift the next time we meet?

Connie agreed. The following day, the dean's assistant called Connie's assistant and mentioned that the dean was once again planning to be in Connie's city and that the development officer would be traveling with him. Without hesitation, Connie's assistant offered several opportunities for a breakfast meeting.

The dean and his development officer debated several approaches to soliciting Connie. To date, Connie had never given any gift to the university. They considered starting with an introductory gift at the high end of their annual giving society. They discussed asking for a major gift at a modest amount, perhaps $25,000. In the end, they decided that Connie would expect to be asked for a very large gift. She had shown that she considered herself to be a superstar, and they decided to make a superstar ask. They decided to ask for $1 million to endow a fund that would nurture students like her: those with significant talent combined with significant financial challenges. They discussed whether to engage the president of the university in the solicitation, but decided that the dean's relationship with Connie was strong enough to carry the solicitation.

When they met with Connie, they began by discussing her day on campus. They shared comments they had heard from students and faculty, all of whom had been thrilled to interact with her. She seemed genuinely pleased to hear of these reactions.

The dean began the solicitation:

> As we parted last time, you agreed that we could bring you some gift ideas. I hope that's still on your mind.

Connie nodded, so he continued:

> The success you've achieved is an excellent example for our students. You saw that they were enthralled with your story. You inspired them during that visit. I know that a lot of them have now raised their expectations about what they can accomplish, based on your story.

Then he addressed what he and his development officer believed was Connie's top personal priority:

> I believe in those students, just as your professors and the donors who provided your scholarships believed in you. I would like you to join me as a partner in investing in their future success.

He paused to gauge Connie's reaction. She said, "What do you have in mind?" He replied:

> A $1 million endowed scholarship fund for students with the highest entering grades and test scores, coupled with the highest demonstrated financial need.

He then stopped talking. Connie did not immediately respond, but he maintained his silence. Finally she smiled and said, "I guess I blinked. Okay, I'll do it. Can the students all be women?"

The development officer and Connie discussed the tactical follow-up that would be needed to establish the documentation for the fund and to transfer stock to establish the corpus.

As the group shook hands at the end of their meeting, Connie smiled and said, "Here's to the start of something good!"

Part Three

Development Program Components

12

Communications

Communications and marketing are vast areas that encompass much more than your development program. Although our focus here is on development communications, it is important to remember that everything your constituency sees, hears, or reads about your college influences their opinions of your program.

Context for Development Communications

Your development communications must be surrounded by an effective overall communications program. If you expect these communications to carry the full weight of your exchanges with your constituents, their effectiveness as fundraising support devices will be diluted. Without a broadly implemented communications program paving the way for discussions about giving, your development staff will have to market your program to one potential donor at a time.

As the leader of your program, you should be able to articulate your mission, vision, goals, and plans. You should also have a clear set of characteristics that make your program distinctive from similar programs at other universities. Your communications about giving will be derived from these basic messages. If you have not yet settled these core issues, you should do so before attempting to devise a development communications program.

Development communications are distinctly different from other forms of marketing and communications such as admissions and recruiting tools. The scarcity of staff resources leads many units to have a single staff member who is responsible for all forms of marketing and communications. If this is your structure, and if this person does not have previous experience in development communications, it would be wise to provide him or her with some education in development. This can be in the form of an overview conference, or you may find that your central development office has an orientation program that can serve this purpose.

Development officers generally have good communication skills. It can be tempting to take advantage of those skills by giving your development officer communications responsibilities. Remember that every time you add components to the development officer's portfolio, you take away time that could be spent on fundraising.

You and your staff will use your development messages in a variety of media: annual giving mailings, brochures and publications, e-communications, speeches, internal communiqués, and your Web presence. In every case, your development messages should be easily recognized as being aligned with and consistent with your other messages. Essentially your development messages are an extension of your core messages, focusing more narrowly on the role philanthropy plays in your program.

Common Development Communications Vehicles

A comprehensive development communications program comprises a combination of materials that are solely dedicated to development content and development components of materials with another primary focus. Throughout all of your communications, you can convey the role of philanthropy in the success of your program. Noting donor support on an event announcement or reporting on development successes in your general communications conveys that everything you do is connected to donor support to some degree.

Your Web site should feature a link to a development site. This may be as simple as a single page delivering your case for support. If you have the resources to create and maintain more complex content, this site can feature multiple pages conveying multiple facets of your development messages. In either case, there should be an obvious link to make an online gift.

There will be a development Web site at the campus level as well. Your development officer should work with the central communications group to ensure that your program is visible on this site. You may be able to provide content for the stories of development opportunities and outcomes. There should be a link directly to your program's development site. If the online gift processing system is operated at the campus level, request that the option of directing a gift to your program be easy to find and use.

Printed materials may include case statements, brochures on special projects, annual giving mail solicitations, and donor cultivation and stewardship publications. Every printed piece should be recognizable as part of an overall package of materials. Consistency in graphic presentation and in messaging helps create a cumulative effect that reinforces your case for support. You may have other publications, such as an alumni magazine or an industry newsletter, where development messages can be appropriately included.

Almost anything that can be printed can also be produced in electronic form. Your constituency may appreciate receiving electronic communications rather than printed communications. E-communications are less expensive to produce and minimize the amount of paper you add to the piles in your constituents' mailboxes. The problem with e-communications tends to be the quality of your e-mail database. If you do not have e-mail addresses for your entire constituency, you will miss many of them by relying solely on electronic distribution of your publications.

Social media can play a valuable role in your communications program. This is an emerging field that changes rapidly, so the possibility is strong that any advice I might offer on social media techniques would be obsolete by the time this book is printed. Tread carefully into new media, investing strategically. Staff this area with someone who already knows the field, not someone who would like to learn. The rapid evolution of social media makes a staff learning curve a liability. As with all other communication techniques, know your audience well before committing to any plan for a social media presence.

Case Versus Case Statement

The terms *case* and *case statement* are often used interchangeably. They should not be.

Your *case* is the reason donors should want to support your organization. It is brief and can be delivered orally in ninety seconds or less. It should be both persuasive and provocative. The ideal case leaves the listener wanting to know more about the points you have made. It engages the listener and serves as a starting point for further conversation.

Your *case statement* is a visual and verbal expansion of your case. Most commonly you will see a case statement in the context of a campaign. It can also be the primary publication, whether on paper or in electronic form, that provides extended information about supporting your program. A case statement uses your case as its core and expands on it with examples and more information.

Your Case

Your case is the foundation of your development communications suite. Everyone in your organization should know and understand it. They should be able to deliver it from memory. It is the defining message of your development program.

A good case conveys to the listener several key ideas:

- An *inspirational vision for where your program will go*. The vision you convey should be the one that you have developed and your internal community has widely embraced. It is not who you are; it is what you intend to become.

- *The rationale for this vision.* This establishes the importance of the direction you have chosen and begins to engage the listener in wanting to help you achieve your vision.

- *Evidence that your program can achieve this vision.* These are current characteristics and accomplishments that show that your program is well positioned to achieve its vision.

- *What it will take to get there.* This section conveys to your listener the key steps it will take to achieve your vision.

- *How the listener can help.* It closes with a call to action.

A Light-Hearted Example of a Case

Your case can be adapted for various audiences and purposes. Here is a light-hearted example of a basic case for support for an imaginary College of Jewelry.

We intend to be a global force in the field of synthetic gemstones. Naturally occurring gemstones are a diminishing resource. Nearly all of the earth's diamonds, emeralds, rubies, and other classic gems have been mined. Without synthetic replacements, gemstone jewelry will become a rare commodity in future generations. Your grandchildren and later descendants would be condemned to a life without an ample supply of sparkling adornments to bring them joy. We can help you avoid this fate through synthetic gemstones.

Our faculty are already at the forefront of developing formulas for new gemstones of the highest quality and beauty. Our students have an appreciation for jewelry that is unmatched in any other student body. No other college of jewelry is addressing this issue. We can set the pace for the future of jewelry worldwide. To do this, we need to expand our graduate program significantly. We need to add engineering faculty to teach students how to create manufacturing processes for synthetic gemstones and business faculty to create paradigms for this new market. We need fellowships to recruit the most talented graduate students in every field of jewelry: design, manufacturing, and distribution. You can build a sparkling future for jewelry by helping us pursue this direction. Please consider making a significant gift to our program.

This overall case can be used to educate general audiences about your fundraising priorities and be tailored to particular audiences as well. For example, when speaking with an engineer, you might remove the reference to business faculty and add more specifics about the engineering component of your plan. When speaking to a donor who might support graduate fellowships, you could mention faculty only in passing and add more content about what it takes to compete successfully for graduate students.

The call to action at the end can also be tailored to be more specific. For example, if you are delivering this case at an alumni gathering, you could add, "In the coming weeks, we will be contacting you to discuss the details of our fundraising initiative. I hope we can count on you to respond generously."

The content of your case is an important component of laying the groundwork with individual donors for a subsequent major gift solicitation. The case alone does not fully convey the possibilities of a gift or attempt to secure the major gift itself. Rather, it creates the context in which you explore the donor's interests to determine which components of your plans would be the most appealing area for the donor to support.

Beware of several common pitfalls that limit a case's effectiveness. The most common is lack of specificity. Your case should convey your competitive distinction in your field. If your case could apply as readily to another program as to your own, you need to make it more specific. Another common mistake is trying to fit everything you could possibly say into your case. A good case raises questions in the listener's mind. The questions your listener asks should spur further conversation, during which you can share many details. Keep your case strategic and concise so that you can determine which component of it strikes the listener's interest for deeper discussion.

Your Case Statement

You cannot have an effective case statement without an effective case. The case forms the skeleton of the case statement, which fleshes out the case by expounding on each component of it. You use a case statement to provide more supporting material to justify each of the components of your case. Thus it can go into much more detail on each point. Most important, the case statement can include stories and examples that bring your points to life in the minds of your constituents.

An effective case statement is a tool that supports conversation. It can be used in wide distribution to educate your constituency broadly on your fundraising priorities. Development officers often send prospects a case statement in advance of a first meeting to serve as a conversation starter.

A case statement, however, no matter how well it is developed and presented, will not close a gift. It is not a replacement for the interactions that you will have with individual donors as your relationships move toward solicitation. You can have a successful development program without an elaborate case statement.

The use of case statements has evolved as financial resources have diminished and electronic communications have grown in popularity. There are now alternatives to the traditional four-color glossy booklet that are equally effective (possibly more so) and much less expensive. A well-developed Web site enables visitors to learn about the components of your program that are most interesting to them. It can be updated frequently to have an unlimited shelf life. Videos can deliver your messages in entertaining ways. The right vehicle for conveying your fundraising messages will depend on your constituency. Determine how they like to receive information, and create your collateral materials accordingly.

13

Campaigns

Campaigns have become a staple of higher education fundraising. Chances are good that at any given time, your university is either in a campaign, preparing for a campaign, or recovering from a campaign. Campaigns are far too complex to cover in detail in this book. This chapter gives a general overview of campaign principles and how you can use campaigns to the advantage of your college. For more in-depth guides to campaigning, see the Recommended Resources section at the end of this book.

Traditionally the term *capital campaign* referenced drives to fund construction of new facilities. The scope of campaigns gradually expanded. By the mid-1980s, many campaigns were comprehensive in nature, encompassing all funds raised by the university during a defined time period. Although the traditional term is still in use, campaigns now commonly address institutional projects well beyond bricks and mortar. Any targeted, time-limited fundraising initiative can be considered a campaign, with or without a formal designation.

The Role of Campaigns

A campaign is essentially a marketing tool to draw extra attention to an institution's highest fundraising priorities in order to attract increased support during a defined period of time. Our primary donor constituency, alumni, will be engaged with our institutions throughout their adult lifetime. They hear fundraising messages from us year after year over several decades. We hear responses from them across the same long time line through their giving behaviors. Campaigns are an opportunity to alter that dialogue.

The most effective campaigns evolve out of an institutional planning process. The goals identified in a strategic plan lay out where the institution wants to go, whether in a particular area or across the entire institution. The goals in a corresponding campaign lay out what it will take to get there. This approach can energize donor constituencies by giving them a way to show their support of our institutional direction.

A campaign supporting inspirational new directions can be the catalyst that spurs donors to a higher level of giving, whether from annual giving to major gifts, or from major gifts to principal gifts. After the campaign, donors may scale back from their campaign level, but they generally settle at a new giving level somewhere between their precampaign and campaign giving. When another campaign is mounted, probably several years later, they can be spurred on to the next higher level. Across the entire donor constituency, this behavior raises our program performance to a new plateau each time we complete a campaign cycle. Over time, campaigns can increase the sophistication and performance of your development program across the board.

Campaigns can also be an effective tool to address an immediate or unusual need. This can take the form of a fast initiative to respond to a campus disaster, such as when a building burns down or floods. It can also seek giving to take advantage of an opportunity, such as a major challenge grant. Donors may consider giving to such a one-time request in addition to their regular giving. This provides the funds the campus needs while strengthening the donor's engagement with the campus. The feeling of having helped in an emergency or having helped realize an opportunity gives donors a sense of responsibility for the well-being of the campus.

As we have seen, the deeper that connection is, the larger their gifts will be over time.

The high visibility of successful campaigns can lead organizations to believe that a campaign will be the solution to all of their financial problems. Unfortunately, campaigns do not cause new donors to materialize out of thin air, and they do not automatically solve organizations' management problems, especially if it is mismanagement that has created the need for a campaign. And although donors may respond to an emergency appeal once or twice, they will lose faith in the organization if it repeatedly launches campaigns because it is once again on the brink of going under.

University-Wide Versus Program-Specific Campaigns

A comprehensive campaign assumes that all units at the university will be conducting their fundraising activities under the rubric of the campaign. There will be a set of campuswide goals, and each college or unit will set its targets within that overall structure. All units have the opportunity to use the campaign construct to advance their development efforts. Some units may have a more obvious alignment with the goals and may be a higher priority for campus leadership and the central development program.

Sometimes the entire campus is not ready to campaign, but an individual college or unit has a pressing need and a good chance of campaign success. Under those circumstances, the university may choose to endorse a campaign targeted exclusively for that program. This implies that the unit is among the highest funding priorities for the campus. The campaigning unit can expect involvement from the leadership of the campus development program as well as the president.

Whether you expect to be involved in a university-wide campaign or launch your own effort, there are some key issues to keep in mind. The additional visibility that a campaign brings to your program makes it critically important that your effort succeed.

Campaign Readiness

Properly preparing for a campaign requires candid and thorough self-assessment to ensure that you are undertaking the campaign for the right reasons and that you implement the campaign effectively. You, your development officer, and the other senior leadership of your program should consider these questions:

- Why do you want to have a campaign?

- How much money do you hope to raise during the campaign, and over what period?

- How does that compare with how much you are currently raising over a similar period?

- What will it take to increase your development program's performance to a level that will meet this goal?

- How many prospects will you need, and at what gift levels? How many of these have you identified, and on what time line are they likely to give?

Confer with your internal community. Unless you are featuring every component of your program equally in your plans, you may find that the campaign has the potential to create factions within your faculty of haves and have-nots. This may be an unavoidable consequence of investing in your areas of strongest potential. Only you can assess whether the outcomes within your program's culture are acceptable.

The increased results of a campaign require increases in effort. Your existing development staffing may not be able to absorb the extra work. Adding staff may be necessary. As Chapter Two explored, it takes time for the impact of new development officers to be evident in your results. Beyond the time required to recruit and orient them, new officers will presumably be attempting to engage new donors. You may be well into your campaign before you can count on those new contacts for major gifts.

The proportion of your time spent on development will also have to increase. Consider how you will adjust your administration to handle that shift.

In addition to your own self-examination, consult with some of your most committed donors and volunteers. Their assessment of your plans and your likelihood of success can serve as a best-case scenario. If your best donors are lukewarm about the idea of a campaign, it is unlikely that your more distant donors will have a more optimistic view.

Your development officer can provide statistical analyses of your constituency's current giving patterns, paired with projections for the giving levels that will be required to reach your goals. The campaign reference materials in the Recommended Resources section have assessment tools that will help you and your staff develop a ruthlessly realistic understanding of what it will take for your campaign to succeed.

You should ensure that you have fully articulated plans for the projects and programs that will be the focus of the campaign. Donors will want to know what their gifts will accomplish and how your unit will be better as a result of the campaign.

At some point in your planning process, you may have to confront the possibility that the capacity of your development program, even with a significant stretch effort, cannot meet the goals you would like to set. Do not ignore this warning sign. The disappointment of lowering your goals, or delaying the campaign until you have built more capacity, will be less than the disappointment of failing to reach a widely publicized goal.

As you go through these assessment steps, seek the input of the most seasoned development officers on your campus. Their experiences in prior campaigns, both positive and negative, can bring valuable perspectives to your preparation process.

External campaign consultants can be helpful in this process as well. It takes considerable resources to engage campaign counsel over a period of time. You may be able to obtain services of counsel retained by the central development office as part of a campuswide planning process. This can decrease the cost to you while ensuring that the advice you get will be tailored to your place in the larger effort.

Phases of a Campaign

The traditional university-wide campaign spans seven to eight years. More narrowly focused efforts may have much shorter time lines.

Quiet Phase

Most campaigns begin with a quiet phase during which you have not publicly announced the campaign or formally committed to a dollar goal. You use this period to test the assumptions on which you have built your campaign plans. You review your messages with potential supporters to determine whether they are effective. You complete recruitment of volunteers if you have chosen to have a campaign advisory committee.

Most important, during the quiet phase you ask your highest-level prospects to make their commitments. These early gifts help you assess whether the goal you are considering is reasonable. If your best donors give at the high end of what you hoped, that can be a sign that your stretch goal is achievable. If not, it may be wiser to adjust your goal downward.

The quiet phase generally lasts for 25 to 30 percent of the full time frame of your campaign.

Public Phase

The transition from the quiet phase to the public phase is marked by a formal announcement of the campaign. Your public announcement identifies the campaign goal, subgoals for the featured priorities within the campaign, and the time frame for the campaign. It is common to make this public announcement at an event where you also recognize the donors who have made early commitments by featuring the impact of their gifts. Their lead serves as a tangible representation of the impact the campaign will have and can inspire others to participate.

There are various models for implementing public phase solicitations. Some suggest working down the gift levels consecutively, focusing on larger gifts at the beginning of the public phase and expanding to solicit the broad constituency for small gifts only near the end of the campaign. Other models recommend a full rollout at the beginning of the quiet phase, encouraging donors both large and small to participate throughout this phase. Your development partners will advise you on the most appropriate model for your circumstances.

Occasionally circumstances arise in the course of the public phase that prompt you to change your goal and time line. These can be positive circumstances, such as gifts coming in much higher than you anticipated. If you are confident that your constituency has more potential and that your donors find the campaign appealing, you can consider adding priorities within the original framework for your goal. For example, if your original goal was to secure 100 new scholarships, you might raise that to 120 or 150.

There can also be negative circumstances that affect your goal. Unexpected events, such as an economic downturn, may hamper your ability to reach your goal on time. In this case, you and your development colleagues will have in-depth conversations about the right course of action. It is more common to extend the time frame than it is to lower the goal. The right decision for your campaign will depend on a number of factors, including the capacity of the prospect pool and the receptivity of your donor and volunteer constituencies to adjusting the terms of the campaign.

Closure

The campaign ends with another public announcement, this time of the successful conclusion of the campaign. This may be in the form of an event or a widespread communication. This announcement should share the outcomes the campaign has funded and should congratulate and thank donors for all they have accomplished.

There is commonly a wrap-up period beyond the end date of the campaign. This time is used for final accounting and documentation of commitments.

Volunteers

A volunteer advisory group can raise the visibility of your campaign among potential supporters. The volunteers' endorsement and participation convey to their peers that this is a worthy effort. If you do not already have a leadership volunteer committee, you can use a campaign-focused group as a trial run to determine whether you would like to create an ongoing board after the campaign. Within the context of an existing advisory board, a subcommittee for the campaign can be a way to recruit new members who have an interest in development. A campaign can help solidify the board's focus on and role in fundraising.

Refer to Chapter Seventeen for more in-depth material on boards.

Operational Considerations

A successful campaign requires strategic investment of resources. The need for additional fundraising staff to increase the number of donor relationships in your program is obvious. There are less obvious, but equally important, investments you should be prepared to make.

Fundraisers are not self-contained income-producing units. They rely on prospect researchers to help them identify potential donors. They need gift processors and data managers to ensure that gifts are properly shepherded once they arrive. They need program support from communications and donor relations staff.

Some of these functions are probably funded and managed in the central development office. A university-wide campaign may include staffing increases in the central program, and these will probably be adequate to serve your needs as well. If you are the only college campaigning, you and your development officer should present central management with projections for the additional services you will need.

You should also be prepared for your nondevelopment administrative staff to absorb additional work. There may be new scholarships to assign and spending accounts to manage. Your increased time commitment to development during the campaign will result in more of your administrative work's being delegated to others within your program. It may or may not be possible to absorb these additional activities within your existing staff structure.

Communications and Events

In addition to the general principles of these two areas, covered respectively in Chapters Twelve and Fifteen, are a few additional considerations to keep in mind for communications and events that are specifically campaign oriented. Chief among these is featuring campaign messages in every communications vehicle and at every event throughout the campaign. Repetition of these messages will embed them in your constituents' knowledge base about your program and prepare them for campaign solicitations.

Communications

As you develop the messages for your campaign, keep in mind that they will be the framework for your development communications for the duration of the campaign. Snappy catchphrases can be appealing when they are first revealed, but wear thin over several years of repeated use. Choose core messages that can be expanded on in multiple ways. This will keep your communications fresh over the several years of campaigning.

As you develop a marketing plan for the campaign, include your internal constituency as an audience. It is important for them to know the rationale for the campaign and how the funds will be used.

Your initial materials will focus on the plans you are implementing and how the gifts raised will support them. These early communications will have a somewhat heavier focus on the program than on donors, as there will be relatively few donors at that stage. As quickly as possible, move toward communications that focus on what donors are accomplishing with their gifts.

Consider your constituency as you are developing your communications plan. If your campaign is targeted toward major gifts, what effect will the publicity surrounding these gifts have on your annual donors? Might they come to wonder whether their small gifts are still important? It may be wise to segment your communications during such an effort. Emphasize ongoing messages regarding the importance of annual giving with those donors, while featuring major gifts in vehicles targeted toward prospects with the potential to give at that level.

Events

One of the key factors in the success of a campaign is the sense of community and shared purpose the campaign engenders among your constituencies. Bringing donors and volunteers together creates an atmosphere in which this shared enthusiasm can grow.

Thus, you may find that you are holding more events during a campaign period than you otherwise would.

Common Events During a Campaign

- Campaign kickoff and public announcement

- Rollout events for various constituencies

- Rollout events in various regions

- Events to honor donors and announce significant campaign gifts

- Goal increase announcement

- Staff celebrations

- Campaign closure celebration

A college-focused campaign rarely needs all of these events. If you are part of a university-wide campaign, the central development program will mount many of them. You can participate in their events with your donors, saving you the cost of presenting the events yourself.

Taking Full Advantage of the University's Campaign

The techniques we covered in Chapter Three regarding making your program a priority for the central development program, and will cover in Chapter Nineteen regarding making your program a priority for your university leadership, are directly applicable during a university-wide campaign.

In the earliest stages of campaign discussions, convey to the campus chief development officer your interest in playing a role in the campaign. Listen carefully as campaign priorities begin to emerge internally, so that you can align your goals with the overall campaign framework. If you have the leeway to define your own goals, be sure that they are consistent with the general goals being discussed.

You may be expected to adhere to a set of centrally defined priorities. Be assertive with the provost, president, and chief development officer about the importance of including your programs in the overall campaign priorities. Once the campus-level priorities have been identified, be as creative as possible in showing alignment between your priorities and these goals. If the campus leadership sees raising a gift for your program as a way to make progress toward the campaign goals, you will have gained some high-powered help in funding your own priorities.

14

Annual Giving

Chapter Six identified how annual gifts fit into a donor's life cycle of giving. Now we will look at how annual giving fits into your development program and the factors to consider when making annual giving decisions.

The Role of Annual Giving

Annual giving is the foundation on which your program is built. It is generally the entry point for donors, some of whom will spend their entire donor experience in this category. Others will use the annual giving program to get acquainted with your program and begin to express interest in greater support. Thus, a critical role of the annual giving program is to identify donors who appear to have the potential and capacity to give at higher levels. You will probably find that almost every major donor to your program started out as an annual giver.

Annual giving programs tend to focus on the most readily identified constituency available to the program. For most colleges, this is the alumni base. Graduates have a natural affiliation with their colleges and disciplines and are the most likely group to become donors. Annual giving is a vehicle to connect with this group en masse.

The annual giving program, commonly referred to as your annual fund, produces unrestricted dollars. While individual gifts to the annual fund are generally small, a robust annual fund can provide you with significant flexibility in discretionary spending.

Investing in Annual Giving

Despite these positive characteristics of an annual giving program, it has its challenges as well. It is a cost- and labor-intensive program with a relatively low return on investment. It is common in annual giving to have a negative return on attempts to acquire new donors. Even with well-established donors, the costs of securing renewals year after year can be high in relation to the small gifts that result. For an administrator with limited resources and an annual giving program that is not well established, allocating budget to this area can seem unappealing at best.

Yet development professionals encourage making the investment. There is the likelihood that the program will produce major donors in the future. Annual giving materials are an important component of communicating with your constituency about your program, its value, and its needs. These materials plant seeds that may come to fruition this year, next year, or at some point in the future. If you find yourself struggling to identify major gift prospects now, it is likely that your predecessors did not adequately invest in a consistent annual giving program. Your investment now will ensure that you do not similarly hobble your successors. If you are in your position for the next several years, the benefits may become obvious even during your tenure.

Approaches to Annual Giving

In major gifts, every strategy is tailored to an individual, and much of your planning is based on subjective observations and interactions. Annual giving is a field primarily of objectivity. Good annual giving professionals are the masters of data and process. Effective annual giving programs have thorough annual plans, sophisticated data analysis and mining techniques, strict adherence to deadlines, and a complex approach to market segmentation and targeting. It has a great deal in common with direct marketing in other industries.

Many universities deploy their annual giving programs through a blend of college-based and centrally based staff. There can be great economies of scale in centralized data management and vendor relationships.

Some universities have a campuswide annual fund, with donors asked to contribute completely unrestricted gifts. You will not benefit directly from your constituency's participation in this model. You can, however, benefit from knowing which of your constituents has given to the fund, especially at higher levels. Your development staff should have access to these data. You may need to negotiate with the highest levels of your university's development management to secure them.

If you have your own unit-based annual fund, be sure you know how the division of labor between your own staff and the central development office's annual giving staff is handled. Annual giving is labor intensive in comparison to the returns. The more you can take advantage of central technical and logistical resources, the more your staff will be available to focus on higher-return programs.

The one component of the annual giving program that you should not relinquish to the center is the messaging. You and your development officer should confer on the focus of your annual giving appeals each year. Discuss which audiences you want to reach and the messages you wish to convey. Whether your officer or a central staff member crafts the messages, you should play a role in fine-tuning the materials to reflect your individual style and voice.

It is critical for your messages to include information on how annual gifts have been used in the past. While it is easy to identify the outcomes of a major donor's gift, annual donors may feel uncertain as to whether their gifts have had any real impact on your program. Conveying to them the benefits provided to students or faculty from the annual fund is an important component of persuading them to give.

Alumni Participation Rates

The traditional measure of success for an annual giving program has long been the percentage of alumni who give. The percentage of participation is often used as an indicator of alumni satisfaction with their alma mater and is a metric frequently included in grant applications. Many rankings, most notably those of *U.S. News and World Report,* use this figure as one of their assessment criteria.

There are significant difficulties in applying this metric as a satisfaction factor in the realm of large universities. The first is the phenomenon of the expanding denominator. Every year your program produces a large number of new graduates, many of them debt-strapped and facing uncertain job prospects. It can be difficult even to find them during their early years after graduation as they move around for jobs and graduate school. Some schools have had success with student and young alumni giving programs, although these are the exception rather than the rule. These brand-new graduates are generally poor prospects for becoming donors right away, and yet their volume swells the denominator of your participation rate immediately on graduation. Each year you must secure a large number of new donors just to keep your participation at the prior year's level.

Many large public universities are relative newcomers to the development world overall and to annual giving in particular. They lack the benefit of an alumni constituency that has been properly cultivated and tended for generations, and thus is well educated in the value of supporting the annual fund. Students at private colleges and universities are often informed of the role of giving in supporting their experience. They are trained from their earliest days in the program community that someday they should give as well. Attempting to create this sense of connection and duty after graduation is daunting, if not impossible.

Finally, the nature of the student population at large universities may not engender the emotional ties that inspire alumni to want to be part of a giving community. Large public universities often have significant commuter student populations. A commuter student who comes to campus only for classes and does not have occasion to engage in traditional campus life activities is less likely to develop and carry forward the type of connection that alumni of traditional residential programs form.

These factors make attempting to improve participation rates a costly and frustrating process. Increasingly development professionals in large universities are placing much less emphasis on participation rates. Instead they focus on overall giving increases and retention of donors from year to year. This is a valid approach. But do not be surprised if your president still expresses frustration over the participation rate each year when the rankings are published.

Giving Societies

The range between an entry-level annual gift and a major gift is vast. It can take several years of participation in the annual fund for a donor to achieve the interest and capacity to consider a major gift. Giving societies are a technique for recognizing annual donors and encouraging them to increase their gifts toward the major gift level.

A giving society recognizes annual donors at various gift levels. Membership may include benefits, and membership must be renewed each year. A giving society generally has a name that is relevant to the program's nature or history, and there are additional names for levels within the society. The entry level for membership, and the levels at which additional recognition and benefits

Table 14.1 Sample Giving Society Membership Levels

	Small Program	Midsize Program	Large Program
Entry level	$500	$1,000	$2,500
First tier	$750	$2,500	$5,000
Second tier	$1,000	$5,000	$10,000
Third tier		$10,000	$25,000
Fourth tier			$50,000
Fifth tier			$100,000

are provided, should be appropriate to the giving behaviors and capacity of your constituency. Programs with relatively few high-end annual donors may start their societies at a lower level than those with robust, well-established programs or those whose donors have a tendency to give larger annual gifts. Table 14.1 provides examples.

The entry level of the society can be a motivator for annual donors to increase their giving so they can join. Once these donors are in the society, the differentiated levels are intended to motivate them to continue to increase their gifts. Many donors find this type of recognition appealing. Giving societies can be a useful tool for development officers to use in personal solicitation of annual gifts.

These higher levels of giving also work to establish a giving behavior that makes the increase up to a major gift more palatable to the donor. A donor who is already giving $5,000 per year will probably find a $25,000 pledge, to be paid over several years, manageable. By comparison, a donor who is currently giving $100 per year would have to make a major change in his or her giving behavior to attain this level.

If you are considering establishing a giving society, begin by assessing your annual donors' current giving patterns. Look for groupings at particular levels. Common entry levels are $500, $1,000, and $2,500. Make sure that you already have a reasonable number of donors at or near the entry level. You want your first membership list to have some names on it. Identify your largest current annual gift, and establish your highest level in sync with this amount. You can add higher levels as your program grows.

Consider carefully the benefits you offer to members of the society. On the legal side, there are tax deductibility consequences for offering high-value benefits in exchange for gifts. You also do not want to raise concern in your donors' minds about how much of their contribution is being used to produce benefits.

Often the most meaningful benefits to donors are intangible. Access to news and information about the program, opportunities to interact with other donors, and opportunities to meet and hear from faculty and students are rewarding and motivational. Recognition in a published membership list should be your baseline for all members. From there, consider adding one or two incremental benefits at each level of membership. Table 14.2 gives some examples.

As with all other development programs, remember to plan for the expense of establishing and maintaining the giving society. Direct costs might include publishing a membership list (this can be an insert in one issue of your regular publication), creating and printing informational materials on the society and levels for membership, mailings to members, and benefits you provide. Indirect

Table 14.2 Sample Benefits Structure

	$1,000	$2,500	$5,000	$10,000
Listed in honor roll	X	X	X	X
Receive donor magazine	X	X	X	X
Invited to annual donor dinner		X	X	X
Invited to reception with president			X	X
Invited to meet speakers and visiting dignitaries				X

costs are primarily the staff time required to track membership, create the published membership list, and implement membership benefits.

More Information

Although annual giving is the most fundamental program, it may be the most technically sophisticated component of our work. The science of annual giving is complex, fascinating, and far beyond the scope of this book. For an in-depth look at the intricacies of annual giving, refer to the Recommended Resources section.

15

Events

Events can be a useful tool in your development efforts. They can also be a significant waste of time and money. Keeping them more the former than the latter takes careful planning on your part and the part of your development officer.

We consider events first by logistical category, then by type and strategic purpose.

Categories of Events

The category over which you have the most control is events that your program puts on for its own benefit. You and your team determine the purpose, the venue, the budget, the invitation list, the program, and all the logistics.

You have less control, but may have input, over the second category: events put on by your university. Campuswide events, such as awards dinners or donor recognition events, may include representation on the program of multiple units. In this case, you can create an opportunity for your unit by lobbying to have content from your area included. You may also have some input into the guest list. You should be invited to attend, and you will have access to information about those who attend.

Events put on by other units offer you opportunities for cultivation activity with your prospects, though you may have no input into the event at all. For example, if one of your donors has an interest in rare books, you might invite that donor to join you as your guest at a reception put on by your university library to unveil a new acquisition. Athletic and cultural events on campus also provide venues for you to have social time with your donors, volunteers, prospects, and alumni, even though you play no official role in the activity.

The final category, other organizations' events, may provide you with selected opportunities to engage with your donors, either because you attend an event where they are also present or because you invite them to attend as your guests. You can also ask your advisory board members and key donors to host your attendance at such events as a way to make new contacts. They may enjoy introducing you to their associates and feel good about helping you expand the visibility of your program.

Types and Purposes of Events

The category of an event is the "what." The strategic purpose is the "how" and "why." In the context of your event work, you will encounter several common types of events, each of which can be used for a variety of purposes.

Large-scale events are often used for broad purposes, such as building a sense of community among your constituency, raising awareness of your programs, building pride among a selected community, offering recognition for constituents' generosity or achievements, or raising money through many relatively small gifts. The invitation list is long, with a wide variety of constituencies included. The impact on your development work of large events is broad, not deep. You will see a lot of people, but you will not have private or deep conversations with many of them. Often these events are university-wide. This exposes each unit's constituents to other university constituents and programs. Examples of large-scale events are campaign kickoffs, alumni awards ceremonies, and homecomings.

Topic-specific events are midsized events that target a narrower group of constituents with common characteristics or interests. Although these events may address the same types of purposes as large-scale events, the content will be more narrowly focused. Many of the events your program puts on will fall into this category. At this size of event, you will be able to meet and talk personally with each guest and will have time for longer, more involved interactions. Examples of topic-specific events are your own program's donor recognition event, a faculty investiture, or a college-specific reception for alumni in a defined region.

Finally there are narrowly focused events that include a small number of guests and are oriented toward a very specific outcome. A common example is a dinner party for several major gift prospect couples to share with them your fundraising priorities or introduce a new member of your faculty whose work you hope they will support.

In Chapter Thirteen, we looked at how the various types of events can fit into your overall campaign strategy.

Using Events Strategically

Events can be expensive, and executing them well is time-consuming and labor intensive. Many new unit heads inherit a tradition of a standing annual event that over time has become a significant drag on program resources without any quantifiable positive outcomes. Similarly, new unit heads often find themselves going to events several times a month without a clear sense of why they are giving up so many of their evenings and weekends.

The key to success in the events realm, as in many others, is to define a strategy for your involvement. This applies to events you are considering putting on, as well as to events you might attend.

When you consider mounting an event, begin by defining clearly what this event is intended to accomplish—for example:

- Provide an engagement opportunity for the guests

- Raise awareness of some component of your program

- Raise money

- Publicize giving opportunities

- Honor those who have given

- Inspire those who have not given

- Reward members of your community who have had significant achievements

Once you have defined the purpose, determine what it will take to achieve this purpose:

- What will be the costs?

- Will the costs be offset by revenues?

- Where will you get the money to fund the event?

- How much staff time will be required?

- Do you have adequate content for a program to achieve your stated strategy?

Careful and candid consideration of these questions will often show that the event idea is not worth pursuing. This can be an especially important process when you have volunteers who suggest having an event. Rarely will they have adequate knowledge of your resources to know whether their idea is realistic. Walking them through these questions will help them better understand why you can or cannot implement their ideas.

Fundraising Events

A significant misconception about fundraising events is that they always raise money. Granted, sometimes they do. But often the appearance of having raised money is illusory. Think about the major fundraising galas in your community. Usually you hear, "We raised $500,000 in one night!" What you rarely hear is what it cost to raise that $500,000. To measure the actual financial benefit of an event requires subtracting a number of things from the gross proceeds:

- Costs of putting on the event, including catering, decor, space rental, and audiovisual.

- Costs of producing collateral materials, including invitations, program handouts, and program content, such as videos.

- Salaries and wages paid to staff while working on the event (both permanent staff who are deployed to the event and any extra help hired for the event).

- Opportunity costs related to staff. For instance, if your development director spends one hundred hours working on an event, that is one hundred hours not spent on major gift work.

A fundraising event may be a cultivation step in some of your major gift relationships. Assess carefully how the progress made in those relationships at the event compares to the progress that could have been made if your development officer had expended the same number of hours working directly with the prospects.

For a fundraising event to be truly financially successful, you will probably have to secure sponsors to underwrite most or all of the costs of the activity. This guarantees that all of your ticket sales, silent auction proceeds, and other revenues will net to your cause. It also allows you to assure your guests that everything they spend on or at the event goes to the cause they are supporting. As you think about who might sponsor an event for you, be sure to determine whether these sponsors might give equivalent amounts directly to your program. Some would. In that case, you can have a direct impact on your programmatic goals without expending staff and volunteer time and resources on putting on an event. Others would not. They use their sponsorship of events to raise their profile among attendees, and thus would see more benefit to their goals in a sponsorship than in a direct program gift.

An engaged and committed volunteer corps can also be a factor in making an event successful. Fundraising galas are often put on by affiliated groups, such as boards, committees, or associations. If you are mulling over engaging such a group to support a fundraising event for your program, assess how much staff time will be required to support the volunteers in their efforts. You may find that no significant salary savings can be achieved through the volunteers' involvement. Although they may not save you much money on the costs side, volunteers can significantly increase the revenue side of an event. If they use their networks and connections to engage high-potential attendees who would not have otherwise participated, their value can be significant.

It is important to convey directly and subtly to guests the role that the event plays in your overall fundraising and program strategy. If the event is to be lavish, feature your sponsors prominently to ensure that guests know you are not spending program money on the event. Identify what connotations the nature of your event may convey: a sumptuous feast to raise money for hunger causes, for example, can cause discomfort among your guests.

Clearly communicate how the proceeds from the event will be used. Ideally they should be targeted to a demonstrable outcome within your program. This will provide good content to share in future communications as you highlight the impact of the funds from the event, and it lays the groundwork for a positive reception to future events you hold.

In collateral materials and program presentations, give the overall context in which this event occurs. Emphasize other components of your fundraising program as well. This will help donors understand that purchasing a ticket to your event is not the only way to support your program. It may decrease the chance that they will feel they have done all they need to do by attending.

Often the true financial outcomes of a fundraising event are realized after the event. Assuming that the event was well produced, your guests will leave in high spirits with a good feeling about your program. It is critical to ensure that everyone who attended receives a personal follow-up from a volunteer or a staff person to capitalize on that enthusiasm. Whether through a direct solicitation in the weeks following the event, or merely a significant cultivation step in the form of a visit after the event, this strategic follow-up increases the likelihood that an event is ultimately profitable.

Making the Most of Your Attendance At Events

At your own program's events, you are clearly the host and one of the most important people in the room. The guests attend because of their interest in you and your program. Your role is to ensure that their experience at the event deepens that interest.

Prior to the event, confer with your development officer regarding seating of key donors. Review the guest list to familiarize yourself with who is attending. At the event, make a point of interacting personally with every guest. During the reception, chat briefly but meaningfully with each guest you encounter, and then move to the next. As interesting as each guest may be, you cannot afford to spend long periods of time in any one conversation. The result would be to ignore other guests and create ill will with them. Your donors will understand that as the host of the event, you cannot devote yourself entirely to them at that time. If a conversation is going well but you need to move on, you can exit gracefully by saying something to the effect of, "I'm thoroughly enjoying talking with you, but I don't want to ignore the other guests. Could we continue this conversation over dinner sometime soon?" This covers your departure and creates an opportunity for a further cultivation step in the near future.

Your development staff can help ensure that you have a direct encounter with every guest. During reception periods, staff can bring donors to you to talk. During seated dinner periods, begin by talking with each guest at your own table. Then excuse yourself and move from table to table greeting everyone you have not already seen. Imagine yourself as the bride or groom moving through a wedding reception dinner.

The staffing plan for all of your events should delineate who is responsible for every component of the logistics during the event. You should not spend any time on tactical matters at the event. All of your focus should be on your guests and your formal role in any program included in the event.

Many central development offices and alumni associations put on campuswide events that can assist you in your relationships with donors. You should be present at most, if not all, of these events. Generally these events have little or no cost to you. They provide a free or low-cost cultivation opportunity of which you should take full advantage.

Including Your Donors in University-Wide Events

Your development officer will often have the opportunity to recommend guests for the invitation list. You and your development officer can make calls or send e-mails to reinforce the invitation and encourage your constituents to join you at the event. Once the responses are in, your officer can usually obtain the guest list to determine which of your constituents are attending. He or she can attempt to have you seated with guests who have a connection to your programs.

Manage your encounters with guests at receptions and dinners of this type just as you would at your own. The difference will usually be one of scope. If the entire university is participating, your program will likely have a small percentage of the overall group of guests. This can make it difficult to find your people. However, you and your development staff will have many fewer responsibilities at this type of event and can spend more time seeking out the important conversations for you to have.

16

Corporations and Foundations

This book has primarily addressed relationships with individual donors, because these will make up the vast majority of your development portfolio. Although most corporate and foundation funding relationships will be handled by your development staff and individual faculty, you can expect to become involved with these donors from time to time. You will find these relationships to be fundamentally different from those you build with individuals.

Institutional Giving Approaches

I have emphasized the role of emotions in gift decisions when you work with individuals. We look for donors' passions and consider their values. If we do not capture the individual's emotions, we are unlikely to get the best gift. With institutional donors such as corporations and foundations, emotion is rarely involved in giving decisions.

Institutional funders operate within established guidelines that define their giving practices. These guidelines are usually inflexible. In the case of corporations, management must answer to stakeholders and cannot appear to be dispersing corporate funds capriciously. Foundations must adhere strictly to their by-laws to maintain their tax-exempt status.

Corporations commonly give through private foundations they have established. The corporate foundation reports to the corporation, and its giving guidelines are either mandated by, or at the very least approved by, corporate leadership. Giving priorities are usually overtly linked to the business interests of the corporation. For example, energy companies may give to sustainability efforts, and manufacturing companies frequently give to civic causes in the communities in which they have facilities.

Private foundations make their gifts out of the income from their invested endowments. They are required by taxing authorities to pay out a defined percentage of the value of their corpus each year. Their giving guidelines are established when the foundation is formed. Large professional foundations have extensive administrative infrastructure supporting their grant making. Foundations established by families or individuals to manage their giving tend to be smaller in both staffing and giving capacity.

Developing Giving Relationships

The pragmatic nature of institutional giving provides your staff with easy access to information on giving levels, priorities, and process. The donor cycle is thus significantly compressed:

- The *identification* stage involves searching any number of easily accessible databases that catalogue institutional giving programs.

- The *qualification* stage involves reviewing the guidelines to see whether your programs fall within them.

- The *cultivation* stage rarely exists; at most, it may involve contact between your staff and theirs to establish that a proposal is on its way.

- The *solicitation* is typically done in writing, without any face-to-face discussion.

- The *stewardship* phase is similarly unemotional, usually comprising submission of written reports on an annual basis.

The relationships that you and your colleagues develop will be with paid staff members of the corporation or foundation. The staff members may bring passion and emotion into their work, but they are not the ultimate decision makers. Tapping into their passions will not open new giving possibilities, as might occur with individual donors. These relationships may also be transitory as the staff members move on to other jobs.

These institutional donors provide an excellent opportunity for your faculty and development staff to collaborate. Development staff can serve as matchmakers, connecting program officers with your faculty who are working in their area of interest. The faculty and development staff can collaborate on funding proposals, each providing content from their areas of expertise. Together they develop a relationship with the program staff that can span multiple gifts and can weather staffing changes within the donor organization.

Finding the Right Opportunities

The key to securing institutional gifts is to scour your programs to find every possible alignment with the donor's established priorities. The program staff in the foundation or corporation must justify their giving recommendations to their boards. Your goal is therefore to provide these staff with giving opportunities that will provide maximum results in their areas of interest.

These ideal opportunities usually involve your faculty members' research work. Encourage your faculty to take an entrepreneurial approach to identifying private funders, with the important caveat that they must keep the development office informed of their activities. As with individuals, we make poor impressions on institutional funders when we bombard them with competing requests and appear not to have effective internal communication.

In Chapter Twenty, we discuss collaborating across college lines to present combined projects to donors. This type of interdisciplinary approach is attractive to institutional funders, as these projects address the funders' priority areas from multiple perspectives simultaneously.

Corporations can also be sources of scholarship support, particularly if you are educating students the corporation would someday like to hire.

Logistical Issues

Often the funds you receive from foundations and corporations come in as grants, not gifts. Universities differ in their practices regarding whether to include these in philanthropy totals. It is important for you to know your university's policy regarding these funds. If they are not included in development totals, you may not be able to deploy your development staff to pursue these contributors.

You must also be certain to have staff in your financial management operation who are familiar with administering private grants. These grants may differ significantly from federal grants, particularly in the follow-up reporting requirements.

Special Opportunities

Large professional foundations often identify areas in which they hope to have a broad societal impact. They may form consortia of organizations working in their area of interest to extend the impact of their gifts. They will sometimes take on a public policy role. If your programs align with such an initiative, you may be able to create a partnership at the highest level of the foundation's management wherein you advise and inform the foundation's activities. You and your development officer should stay carefully attuned to such possibilities. Although they do not arise frequently, when they do, they are excellent opportunities for funding and for visibility for your programs.

Corporations may give weight in their decision-making process to your university's presence within their employee body. Your development officer can obtain information from the university's database regarding alumni employed at the corporation. The corporate giving staff may be able to identify additional graduates who are working at the corporation but have not updated their business information in your database. You and the other academics whose alumni have significant representation among this group can host a reception for all of your alumni at the company. Corporations often host these receptions as a goodwill gesture for their staff. This helps raise your visibility within the corporation. It gives you an opportunity to engage with alumni you were not previously reaching. If you have alumni who are highly placed within the corporation, they may become advocates for you internally—for both giving possibilities and other opportunities, such as research contracts and student job placement.

17

Advisory Committees

An advisory board can be a significant asset to your program in fundraising and well beyond. Volunteers who are deeply engaged in your program and committed to your leadership will expand your network of advocates and help you accomplish things you and your staff cannot do alone. Membership on a board is an excellent way to deepen a donor's understanding of and engagement with your program. And along the way, your board just might give you some good advice.

If your reaction to that idea is, "But what if I don't want any advice?" you are not alone. Academic leaders often worry that a board will become intrusive into the running of their programs. The key is to define what type of advice you ask your advisory board to give. That will determine the type of board you establish.

Types of Boards

It is rare for a unit within a university to have a board with true legal governance responsibilities; these are almost always positioned at the university level. Without formal governance responsibility, unit-level boards can play many different roles. Let's look at a few of the most common types.

True Advisory Board

A true advisory board, with the right membership, can offer you an important window into how external constituencies are thinking and feeling, and not just in the development realm. You may be comfortable having a group of volunteers who offer advice on key issues in your program. They can be a sounding board for new ideas and a source of expertise to help you consider how to address problem areas. Even with such a comfort level, it is wise to guide the board toward areas where they can be of most assistance to you. A surefire way to demoralize a group of volunteers is to ask them for advice again and again and never take that advice. Avoid this by never asking for advice in areas that are not up for discussion. Examples of these forbidden areas might be issues of tenure, academic freedom, and admissions standards.

Development Board

A fundraising board has a narrowly articulated focus and can be a powerful component of your development program. Their input may expand into other areas, but their key focus is to help you raise more money. Members would be recruited from among your best and most loyal donors. They may offer ideas about and insight into initiatives you are considering, and they should both give themselves and solicit, or help you solicit, others.

Corporate or Industrial Board

Your academic area may lend itself to assembling a board of experts in your field. In fact, some disciplines require such a group for accreditation purposes. This type of board can sometimes lead to fundraising and other financial opportunities, but that is not its main focus. Members might serve on this type of board based on their professional status, and thus may move off the board if their job circumstances change. For example, an engineering college might establish the practice of always inviting onto its board the head of research and development from a major corporation in its region. When the holder of that position changes, the representation on the board could change too.

Project-Focused Board

Typically these boards have a tightly defined focus, such as serving as the organizing committee and judging panel for a student competition. The group would exist for a finite period of time as warranted by the nature of the project and then be dissolved. This type of volunteer group can be a good way to test whether your program would benefit from having a more formal ongoing volunteer structure.

What to Call Your Board

Advisory boards are called by many names: visiting committee, board of visitors, industrial advisory board, alumni board, campaign committee, and so on. Before you decide on what to call your group, look around your university to determine whether there are norms on your campus. Ask the development office if campus policies or preferences address naming volunteer groups. Especially check on whether it is permissible to use the word *board* if you are so inclined. In some universities, there is sensitivity to using that term too broadly because it applies to the one true board: the governing board of the university. If you are at a public university, using the term *board* may subject you to sunshine laws and other regulatory matters that are best avoided. In that case, consider using *committee* in your group's name.

Starting a New Board

Begin by articulating clearly what you want from your board. This is a time to be completely candid with yourself and with those who may be helping you put your board together. Say what you want and, more important, what you do not want your volunteers to do. You may want professional advice, a "kitchen cabinet," external

advocacy, or a particular type of expertise. This list can be whatever you want it to be as long as it is thorough and frank.

Start with a steering group of your strongest supporters by
asking them to join you for a brainstorming conversation. Let them
know that you are considering establishing a volunteer group and
that you would like their perspective. These should be people who
know you and your program well and have experience
serving on other high-level volunteer groups. Host them for dinner,
and share with them what you hope to gain from having a board.
Listen carefully to their thoughts and advice. You may find that
out of this initial brainstorming conversation, some of these friends
will volunteer to serve on the board and help to recruit other
members.

Before you recruit your first official member, put some infrastructure in place. The right volunteers will want to know how the
board is going to work and what will be expected of them. Draft a
mission or charter for the group. You probably do not need formal
by-laws, since this is not a true governing board, but you should
include in this document the purpose of the group, how often it
will meet, and members' responsibilities.

Prepare a written job description for members. Your prospective members will want to consider carefully whether they can
meet the expectations of the position. A written job description
helps ensure that there are no surprises after they have agreed
to join. The job description should begin with a statement of
purpose for the board—why it exists and what role it plays for
you and your program. Then you should articulate the following
points in it:

○ *The terms of membership.* Decide how long a term on the board
lasts, whether the terms are renewable, and whether there are term
limits. Defined membership terms, with limits, are a benefit for
you and for your volunteers. The term assures them that they are
not committing to a lifelong responsibility, and it offers you a

graceful way to rotate off members who are not fulfilling their responsibilities.

○ *Meetings and attendance expectations.* Identify how many meetings will occur each year, and whether members must attend in person or can participate by teleconference or videoconference. Although defined terms afford you the means to remove a board member who is not participating, you may also want to include a provision that membership on the board is automatically revoked after a set number of absences.

○ *Giving expectations.* I believe board members should be expected to give to your program every year. Although their time is a gift in itself, volunteer service does not pay your bills. It is likely that other boards on which they serve expect giving, and they probably will not be surprised that you require it as well. You might set a base amount that every member should give. Some program heads direct these board membership gifts into a discretionary purpose for their own projects. Others identify a common interest, such as scholarships. Some encourage the members to make their gift to any area of the program. And some academics use these baseline board contributions to fund the workings of the board itself. You will likely have a membership with a wide array of giving capacity. In that case, the required board gift should be a minimum. Those with significant additional capacity should be encouraged to give well above this level. If you decide not to require giving, be aware that if you ever decide to change this, it will be a tough process. Most development officers have had to address this issue with an inherited board, the stance of which is, "But I was told I would never be solicited on this board." Think carefully before you put yourself, or a successor, in that position.

○ *Any other requirements.* If you expect your board to attend certain events or participate in particular activities, list them here.

Your members should come onto your board with a full understanding of the time commitment they are making.

Consider customizing one section of the description for each recruit. Use this area to describe the particular expertise you hope the recruit will bring to the board. This will show the recruits that you have thought strategically about the board, and they will see this as an indication that joining the group will be a meaningful and worthwhile experience.

Decide how you will staff the board and pay for its operation. Though we do not pay them salaries, volunteers are not free. Someone has to plan and execute the meetings, including creating and distributing advance materials, monitoring attendance, arranging for a meeting space and catering, preparing materials to be used during the meeting, and implementing appropriate follow-up steps. Often the staffing of the board falls to the development office. This can be an appropriate assignment for development staff, especially if one of the purposes of your board is to cultivate deeper relationships with major donors and prospects. Keep in mind, however, that time spent planning and executing board meetings is time taken away from major gift fundraising. The trade-off may be appropriate and worthwhile. Just be sure to acknowledge this choice and incorporate it into your expectations for your development staff's performance.

The budget for a board does not have to be large. You can often hold the meetings in space you control and thus need not pay for. But there are operational costs, such as making copies and sending out advance materials. You will probably provide refreshments, and possibly a meal, for the group.

Recruit a board chair. Although you will occasionally see advisory boards that are chaired by the academic leader, having a volunteer chair is a better choice. A volunteer can interact with board members as a peer, which can be critical if problems arise with members. A good chair can be a partner to you at board meetings and between them, assisting you in developing and nurturing the board into a true asset for your program. Most important, a chair with significant positive name recognition among your constituency sends a message about the importance and relevance of this board. You and your development officer should consider a range of possibilities, ultimately approaching the person who most embodies what you want your board to be and with whom you feel completely comfortable.

Board Members

Now you are ready to begin recruiting members. Start with the group of key supporters who helped you develop a strategy for your board. Your new chair should ask each of them to join the board as a steering committee. An important component of their role will be to help you recruit additional members. This request should come as no surprise to these volunteers, and most of them will agree readily.

Bring your steering committee together to develop a list of potential members. Start by identifying all the characteristics you want to have on your board. There are givens, such as availability, reputation, and established affinity for your program. Then there are characteristics that will be important to your particular program. You may want representation from a variety of departments, taking care to have a representative from each major division or department within your program. Perhaps geographical representation is a distinctive characteristic of your constituency. You may value diversity in various categories, such as age, gender, ethnic background, or national origin.

List your desired characteristics across the top of a grid, like the one in Table 17.1. As you add names to the list, check the boxes that apply to each potential member. Some members will have more than one characteristic: on our grid, a young female marketing executive meets three criteria. This grid will help you avoid

Table 17.1 Sample Recruitment Grid for a Board

	Female Representation	West Coast Alumni	East Coast Alumni	Political Connections	Marketing Expertise	Global Business Experience	First Twenty Years Postgraduation
Martha Smith	X				X		X
José Alvarez		X					
Judith Chang	X		X			X	
Bill Jones				X			X

having a homogeneous membership, and will encourage you to think outside your usual list of volunteers to find new people who round out your mix of characteristics.

Developing this list may take several sessions. As you, your development officer, and your steering committee think about the list between conversations, new names will occur to you to expand your membership.

Once your grid is mostly full, sort the names in priority order. Your first target should be to double the size of your steering committee with high-caliber members. Determine your ideal targets for these positions on your board, and identify who should recruit each one. As a group, agree on a time line to make these recruitment calls and visits. A mutual agreement, with regular check-ins on progress, will keep you all accountable for fulfilling your assignments. Given the stature of your steering committee and your potential recruits, a sixty- to ninety-day window is a reasonable time frame for completing these contacts.

Ideally these recruitments will be done in person. The recruiter should contact the prospect, explain the nature of the request, and ask for an in-person meeting. The meeting can include you, a development officer, and the recruiter, in any combination. At the meeting, the recruiter should share the materials you have developed, including the board member job description and a list of those who have already joined. The prospective member may give you a decision during this meeting. If he or she needs time to think about it, agree on a period of time after which you can call to get an answer.

If some of your early prospects decline, move down the priority list until you have secured the targeted number. At this point, your board should have eight to twelve members. The chair can now call a meeting of this group to get the work of the board started.

Let the group meet at least once, and preferably several times, before moving on to additional recruitment. This allows the culture of the board to emerge and gives you an opportunity to get ideas from this initial group regarding other potential members. The ultimate size of your board will vary depending on the type of board and your expectations for the members. If it is a project-based board where the majority of the work will happen in a short span of time, a smaller group may be more nimble and effective. For a longer-term board, a membership of at least twenty is required to ensure a critical mass of attendance at each meeting. Above twenty-five, the group may become unwieldy, and you and your staff will not have enough time to give each member the attention he or she deserves. Take your time growing to your ultimate size. Allowing the process to evolve organically keeps you on the alert for possible new members who may not have occurred to you in the early rounds of recruitment.

Implementing Term Limits

If you have established term limits, you need to stagger which members are on which terms so that all of your original members' terms do not expire at once. A technique I have used successfully is to put an equal number of slips of paper with the numbers 1, 2, and 3 on them into a hat or bowl. Each board member draws a number, and that becomes his or her "class" on the board. On a new board, those in the class whose membership expires in one year will almost certainly all engage for a second term. This technique can also work with an existing board that has decided to implement term limits and needs to decide which of the long-standing members should rotate off first.

Board Meetings

There is no magical number of meetings you should have each year. Choose what makes sense for you and the makeup of your board. Take into account the geographical distribution of the members and what it will take for them to attend. Be sure you can manage the logistics of whatever number of meetings you set. Preparing for and implementing a good meeting will take a fair amount of logistical work. You have to be prepared for the staff involved to step back from their other responsibilities each time a meeting is on the horizon. Some of the best work of the board happens between meetings as you tap into members' expertise to advise or assist you on particular projects. You can probably accomplish all you need from the assembled group in two or three meetings per year.

The board chair should convene and run the meeting according to an agenda that has been shared with the members in advance. You and your chair should have a series of discussions prior to each meeting regarding what will happen at the meeting and what outcomes are important to achieve.

An ideal meeting is a blend of activities: a showcase of faculty or student accomplishment, a traditional business meeting around a table with discussion of issues, and some social time for the board members. Beginning or ending with a meal or reception can provide an opportunity for the board members to get to know each other personally and coalesce as an engaged group.

If you have significant out-of-town membership, consider timing your meetings to coincide with a university activity. Having an afternoon meeting and then attending a concert or sporting event on campus is more appealing than merely flying in and out for a meeting.

Common Problems with Volunteer Groups

As a new program leader, you may inherit a board established by one of your predecessors. In the best case, the board will be an effective, engaged group that helps you establish your leadership role. If that best case has not happened to you, here are some ideas for solving common problems you may encounter with your board.

Wrong Leadership

The wrong board leadership comes in many forms:

- The power-hungry chair who uses the board for personal benefit

- The uncommitted chair who disappears between board meetings

- The chair who has been in place for many years, either because of being unwilling to relinquish the position or because no one else will do it

- The chair who is not good at running meetings, leaving the group in shambles and the agenda ignored

- The chair who was intensely loyal to a prior administrator and cannot make peace with your arrival

The list goes on, with each example as frustrating as those before it. If you do not have good leadership, your board will never be a true asset. This problem must be resolved before you can move on to shaping the board into the group you need it to be.

The best way to avoid leadership problems is a solid succession planning process. If your board has such a process, you may choose to wait out the term of the ineffective chair. If it does not, this is a good place to begin with solid business practices for your board. Engage your board in a discussion about its structure, and introduce the concept of terms. A good term structure will include defined terms for chairs. If you have relatively few meetings each year, a two- or three-year chair term gives the chair enough time to establish himself or herself and have a positive effect on the board.

If your ineffective chair resists relinquishing the position, you may have to insist on his or her resignation. This is, after all, your board, to benefit you and your program. Before you take this step, be sure you have assessed the culture of the board. What will be the consequences of removing this chair, and are you willing to bear them? You may find that the board members are relieved by the change—or are up in arms about it.

Once you have resolved your current leadership problem, continue with wise succession planning. Always have in mind at least two board members who would be good future chairs. Work with your current and past chairs to identify these rising stars, and engage them in increasingly important activities to assess their leadership capacity. Recruit your next chair at least one year prior to the transition to give time for overlap with the current chair.

Wrong Purpose

You may have inherited a board that was established for a purpose that is not consistent with what you need from a board. Begin by addressing this issue with your chair. If your chair is an appropriate choice to lead the type of board you want, you will have a partner in effecting this change. If not, the chair may voluntarily step down, or you may have to have the difficult conversation referenced earlier.

Determine whom you would like to engage as your new chair, and have a series of conversations with the person about the direction in which you are going. This new chair will be a critical part of communicating the change to the board membership. He or she should be convinced that the direction you are taking is a good one and thoroughly supportive of you before you initiate a discussion with the rest of the members.

You and your new chair should then convene a candid discussion with the board during which you share what you need. Tell the members that you will be coming to meet with them individually to discuss their role in the new structure. Some members will use this occasion to step down, which can be helpful to your transition. For those who wish to continue, explain in detail where you want the board to go and what will be expected of them if they stay on. Those who embrace your new direction will form the core of your new board and can help you with recruitment efforts.

Members Who Need to Go

There are as many versions of bad members as there are of bad leaders. Some are relatively benign, such as those who do not attend or do not participate when they do come to meetings. Others can be poisonous to the board culture. A negative, critical member can make the meetings unpleasant and drive away good members.

One of your chair's responsibilities should be to address membership issues, both good and bad. Your chair should help you recruit new members and take responsibility for terminating members whose presence is no longer desirable.

If you have term limits and only one or two ineffective members, you may feel most comfortable allowing the term limits to solve the problem for you. But if you have inherited a group of members who have a culture that is unacceptable to you, you will have to consider more assertive action. You should consider whether you prefer to "rip the bandage off fast" or "rip the bandage off slowly." There will be significant ramifications with each of these approaches. Whichever one you choose, be prepared to bear the consequences.

The fast approach is to remove all of the inappropriate members at once. If you have a lot of inappropriate members, you probably do not have a good chair, and you will be in this alone. Although the good members may appreciate the change, it is likely to cause a great deal of discussion among your external constituency, led by those who are unhappy to have been removed. Before you implement a mass membership change, develop a core group of supporters who can help you reestablish your board. Follow the guidelines earlier in this chapter regarding starting a new board, and add to your discussions a plan for the membership change and for whatever consequences arise from it.

The slow approach is to gradually replace the inappropriate members over time. This is less likely to produce a volatile reaction from the members. It also prolongs the negative culture on the board. This may make it more difficult to recruit good new members if they are aware of the negative culture. Again you must identify a core group of reliable supporters first and engage them in your plans to evolve the membership of the board. As peers to those you are trying to recruit, they may be able to have candid, confidential conversations with potential new members about the transition process. These conversations should include a request for the new members to take the risk of joining a board that is still a work in progress.

Keeping Volunteers Engaged and Happy

Consider these techniques as you develop relationships with your board members:

- *Do not tell them things they can read.* Send materials before each meeting with routine reports and standard content. Avoid agenda items that consist mainly of you or your staff reporting on subjects that could have been covered in the advance materials.

- *Do not subject them to pointless meetings.* Have meetings only when you have meaty agenda items that engage the volunteers and tap into their expertise.

- *Use them.* Your volunteers agreed to help you. If they do not feel they are contributing something useful, they will leave and go to another volunteer activity.

- *Keep in touch.* Have fewer meetings and more one-on-one interactions. A call to get a volunteer's opinion or an e-mail to tell a volunteer you have implemented one of his or her ideas reinforces that person's importance to your program.

Case Study

The Rewards of Long-Term Relationships

Ben Benefactor graduated with a B.A. in English from Sample University. He went on to a university in another state to earn his M.F.A. in creative writing and made his permanent home in that area. He became a poet and supplemented the income he received from sales of his poems with various teaching jobs. He gained some renown as a poet and secured publishing contracts for three successive volumes of poetry over the course of a decade. This success led to numerous engagements to give poetry readings and to speak at academic symposia.

Ten years after receiving his undergraduate degree, Ben responded for the first time to an annual fund solicitation. He sent a check for $50, requesting that it benefit the English department. He continued to give in response to annual fund solicitations by mail and phone almost every year. The gifts were generally in the range of $50 to $150. The larger gifts were always the result of a phonathon call. If a student reached him, Ben engaged in conversation about the student's classes and campus life. When the student caller would ask for an increased gift, he always agreed. In the years when callers did not reach him, he responded by mail at the end of the calendar year. Those gifts were smaller. Large or small, the gifts were invariably designated for the English department.

Ben's twenty-fifth class reunion year coincided with the publication of his second volume of poetry. His success as a poet had come to the attention of the English department, as had his regular annual contributions. The chair of the department wrote to Ben, inviting him to give a reading and book signing on campus. Ben wrote back to say that if the date for a reading could be coordinated with the dates of the reunion, he would be delighted to participate. He preferred not to make two separate trips back to campus. The chair was happy to oblige, and Ben's reading became a featured activity of the reunion weekend programming.

Ben had a terrific time at the reunion. He reconnected with classmates and saw several of his favorite faculty members. He was flattered by the large crowd that attended the reading and even more flattered by the long line at the book signing.

The annual fund solicitations to Ben's class during the reunion year had requested a special increase in giving in honor of the milestone. Ben had responded before the reunion weekend with a gift of $500. Subsequent to the weekend, he sent another check for $500, along with a note of thanks to the English department chair for the department's hospitality during his visit. In addition to the university's standard receipt and gift acknowledgment, the department chair sent a personal note of thanks.

The following year, Ben responded to the fall solicitation mailing with a $500 check for the English department. Again the department head wrote a personal thank-you note to supplement the university's standard materials. This pattern continued for several years. Now instead of fluctuating between $50 and $150, Ben's gifts fluctuated between $500 and $750. Each time Ben gave, the department chair wrote a note. When the department chair's term expired and a new chair was appointed, the outgoing chair wrote Ben a note introducing the new chair. The new chair followed up with a note as well and continued the practice of sending a special note each time Ben sent his annual gift.

As Ben's thirtieth reunion approached, the development officer for the College of Arts and Humanities contacted Ben. She asked to meet with Ben the next time she was in his area. He agreed, and they met for coffee a few weeks later.

The development officer thanked Ben for his regular annual giving. She asked him about his poetry and publishing, and shared updates from the campus and personal greetings from several faculty members. They talked about the new department chair, whom Ben had not met. Ben commented on how much he enjoyed the notes from the chair each year. During the conversation, Ben told her that he wouldn't be attending the reunion because he had a deadline looming for his next book of poetry. She expressed disappointment on behalf of the university and his classmates and offered to send him a link to a photo site where he could see pictures from the event.

Upon her return to the campus, the development officer met with the department chair. She reported on her meeting with Ben and told the chair that he was preparing another book for publication. They discussed appropriate next steps and decided that the chair would call Ben to congratulate him on the new book.

The chair called and reached Ben's voice mail. He left a message:

Hello, Ben. This is Professor Scott Scholar. I've just been talking with my colleague Adeline Advocate, and she told me about her visit with you last week. What great news that you have another book coming out! I hope you'll consider doing another reading and signing on campus when the book is published.

He left his phone number. A week later, Ben returned the call. He and the chair had a cordial conversation about publishing deadlines and the life of a writer. The chair repeated his invitation for a campus book signing, and Ben agreed. The book was to be published six months later, and they agreed to e-mail regarding schedules once the date grew closer.

Two months later, the chair saw an article in an online journal about the challenges of achieving success as a poet. He e-mailed Ben with a link to the article and a simple note:

I thought of you when I saw this article. You've certainly beaten the odds.

Ben replied with a lighthearted comment about the glamorous life of a starving poet.

The chair responded with a reminder that the department would be pleased to have a reading if Ben was still so inclined. They proceeded with scheduling, and the reading was set to coincide with publication of the book.

A week before the reading, the development officer e-mailed Ben and asked if he would be available to have coffee during his campus visit. He agreed, and they met several hours after the reading and signing. The event had been successful, and Ben was ebullient.

After discussing the event and Ben's visit in general, the development officer asked him for an increased annual gift. She began by thanking him for his prior support:

We are very grateful for your annual contributions. It's a great benefit to the department to have such loyal friends who support the program year after year.

Then she asked for the increase:

Would you consider increasing your gift this year to $1,000?

Ben demurred, saying that while he was supportive of the program, he rarely had $1,000 in disposable income at any one time. The development officer responded with an alternative:

> If you would like to reach the $1,000 level, perhaps you could do so with two gifts of $500 at separate points in the year.

Ben agreed that this was possible. He committed to making one gift in December and another in April, both of $500.

The development officer stayed in touch with Ben, contacting him shortly before each gift date to ask if she could assist in any way. He began sending his checks directly to her rather than to the general address for the annual fund.

Thus began an annual pattern. The development officer would visit with Ben once a year, sometimes in person, sometimes by phone. She would ask for his commitment for the coming year. Every few years, Ben agreed to a slightly larger amount, and they discussed the number of payments Ben would make to fulfill his pledge. The development officer would contact him around the time of each gift to offer her assistance.

Meanwhile, the department chair stayed in contact with Ben as well. In addition to a personal note after each gift, the department chair sent occasional e-mails with news from the program. This continued as the chair's term concluded and another faculty member became the chair.

Over the next fifteen years, the department maintained this regular low-intensity contact with Ben. He came to campus from time to time, and when faculty visited his area, the development office would arrange visits for them with Ben.

At the age of seventy-two, Ben died. Shortly after, the university received a communication from the executor of Ben's estate: Ben had left the university a fully paid life insurance policy for $1 million, designated to the English department. He had also left the department his papers, covering his fifty-year career as a poet. He included a cash bequest of $25,000 to catalogue the papers and establish the collection in the university library.

With the letter from the executor came a note from Ben. He had written it in the last year of his life, expressing his warm regard for the university and his appreciation for the kindness and hospitality the English department had shown him throughout his life.

Part Four

Special Topics

18

Notes for Department Heads, Center and Institute Directors, and Other Academic Leaders

Much of the attention paid to academics in fundraising focuses on deans, often the most visible members of the academic community in the development world. But many others can also play a key role in campus fundraising. The fundamentals covered in this book can be useful to those who are department heads or are the equivalent of academics but in noncollegiate programs—for example:

- Cross-college interdisciplinary programs

- Campus-level centers and institutes

- The university library

- Athletics

- Student affairs

- Performing arts programs and venues

- Museums

Department Heads

Just as fundraising responsibilities trickled down from presidents to academics, they are trickling as well to department heads. Engaging directly in raising private philanthropy has benefits for your program and your professional growth. If you have aspirations to be a dean or any other type of academic leader, developing your fundraising skills now will better position you to be a successful candidate for such a position in the future. At a programmatic level, private philanthropy may be one of the few sources of funds over which you can have direct influence. Engaging in development for your department, within the context of your college's overall development program, will bring in direct support and will position your department as an asset to, and potentially a beneficiary of, your dean's fundraising work.

In Chapter Three, we considered how a senior administrator, such as a dean, can take best advantage of the development programs and resources at the campus level. Substitute "department head" for "dean" and "college" for "campus"; you'll see that you and your faculty can implement nearly every tactic: nest your priorities and messages within your program's priorities and messages, create a partnership with your program development staff, and work to help your dean succeed. This will help make your own department a priority within your college, just as your dean is attempting to make your college a priority for the campus.

Be sure that the dean knows you are interested in engaging in fundraising. The development team follows the dean's priorities, and your goal is to become one of those priorities. Let your dean know that you are going to meet with the development staff to learn from them and explore where your fundraising potential may lie.

Build your partnership with the development staff through regular, constructive encounters. Learn how they approach their work and where their priorities lie. Offer to help them in whatever way you can. They may not be able to deploy staff directly on your behalf, but they can give you suggestions about how to get started within your department. Invite your program's lead development officer to one of your departmental meetings to talk with your faculty as well.

Communicating with your department's graduates is an important foundation for any development efforts. If you do not yet have a departmental newsletter (whether paper or electronic), start one. Use this communiqué to keep your graduates up to date on what is happening in the department and to ask them to engage with you. Some alumni stay in close touch with individual faculty members or their department even while falling off the address lists of the university's alumni and development programs. You may be able to reach potential donors who are not currently receiving any communication from the university overall.

Spend time with your program development staff discussing potential supporters. Suggest names of your alumni who have been successful. Offer to work with the development office to make contact with these graduates and participate in developing relationships with them. When these relationships progress to the point of giving, the donors are likely to direct their gifts to your program.

Keep the lines of communication with the development office open. Tell them what you are doing, and respect the parameters in which they ask you to implement your development work. If you appear to be in conflict or competition with the overall college efforts, donors will feel uncomfortable and may not give. And you will lose out on the useful resource of expertise available to you on that staff. As you lobby your dean for more support for your growing development work, the development staff can be important allies in assuring the dean that an allocation of resources to add staff for you is a good investment.

Like provosts, deans often wish they could see the return on investment before actually making the investment. Your dean may not want to give you funding for your development efforts until he or she is sure these efforts will bear fruit. You will probably have to invest some of your time and resources to get your development activities started. Once you have begun to show success, you may have a case for asking the dean to invest in dedicated fundraising staff for your department. If that time comes, the concepts in Chapter Three can again be translated from the dean's perspective to yours.

Noncollegiate Units and Programs

The primary difference between the development work of a college and that of a unit is the nature of the constituency. The natural development constituency of a college is alumni. The college knows who they are and, to a great extent, where they are. Their affiliation with the college is clear. The college thus has a large pool of potential supporters to attempt to engage without having to identify such a group from scratch.

Some units can readily define their constituency as well—for example, patrons of a campus performing arts center. But the nature of the connection between those constituents and your unit may be quite different from the affinity of a graduate with a college. Alumni often feel they got their start on the path to success by attending college. They credit their university, and their college, with having prepared them for all they have subsequently achieved, a natural foundation for a conversation about giving. Even if you can identify a constituency, it is unlikely that such a deep bond as colleges have with alumni will be present.

For campus service units, such as athletics, the library, and student affairs, all alumni are your alumni, and yet very few of the alumni actually are yours in the usual sense. Students do not receive their degrees from your unit. Even student athletes graduate from a college, not from their sport. Although your program unquestionably contributes to the quality of life on campus and the overall student experience, most alumni do not automatically think of themselves as having a connection to the services you provided for them. You will have to work to remind them of the role you played in their student life and educate them on the value of supporting you now. Meanwhile, your targets are the targets of other programs as well, primarily the college from which they graduated.

Several approaches can help improve your capacity for securing philanthropic support.

o *Work on building partnerships with other units.* Show your fellow leaders how your program adds value to theirs. For example, a robust library helps academics in the recruitment and retention of faculty. State-of-the-art hospital facilities will help the medical school attract better faculty and medical students. Strong athletics programs contribute to a campus environment that students remember fondly when they are alumni. Propose initiatives— whether a strategy for a single donor or a solicitation program for a larger group—that will benefit both your program and one or more colleges. This takes building trust with your colleagues and may not happen quickly.

o *Make your program offerings helpful to others on the campus.* Make it easy and affordable for academics to use your athletic games as entertainment opportunities with their donors and volunteers. Encourage other programs to host events in your facility. Provide experts in your program to serve as speakers at events. This will raise your visibility with donors who participate and will help you stay on the mental short list of interesting programs the campus leaders discuss with donors.

o *Be creative about identifying groups of potential donors.* Parents of undergraduates like to think their children spend a lot of time in the library; affiliate yourself with parents fund activities, or solicit them if no one else is doing so. Graduate students are often difficult to engage as donors because their experience is more like a job than like the emotional ties to the undergraduate experience. Propose that your program solicit graduate students from programs that have a natural tie to your area, and split the returns with the appropriate colleges.

If your program is not in a college and has no direct connection to a development officer, approach the central development office leadership to determine who might be able to help you get your efforts started. The same principles recommended for department heads with respect to college development officers apply here:

- Show your willingness to be entrepreneurial.

- Respect the parameters within which they work.

- Keep them informed of what is going on in your area, and offer to brief the central major gift officers about your program.

In their work with a wide array of prospects and donors, they may encounter individuals who have interests that are consistent with what you do.

19

Engaging Campus Leadership in Your Development Efforts

Just as your involvement in a donor relationship can be instrumental in increasing the likelihood and level of the donor's support, the introduction of a senior campus figure can play a critical role in securing gifts at the highest levels. The presence of the president, chancellor, board chair, or other senior figure communicates both the importance of your program and the esteem in which the institution holds the donor.

The Role of the President

It is likely that your president, or the equivalent top leader, is expected to engage heavily in development. Rarely is this not an overt component of a top executive's responsibilities. By providing your leader with opportunities to assist in securing large gifts, you are becoming a part of his or her success. That will have benefits beyond just the gifts he or she helps you attain.

Bringing a top leader into your relationship with a potential donor creates an opportunity for the donor to hear directly from the highest levels of the university that the program he or she is considering supporting is a high priority not just for you but for the campus. Donors may harbor concerns that if you were to leave, the program they love would not remain a priority for your successor. The assurance from above you that this is an institutional priority, not just your personal priority, can reassure the donor in this regard.

The president can say things about you and your program that you should not say yourself. Consider a situation where you are the dean and one of your department heads is talking with a donor. The department head says:

> "I'm the best in my field."

> "I'm a world-renowned scholar."

> "I'm a great asset to this college."

> "Without me, this department wouldn't be anywhere near as strong as it is."

> "Retaining me and keeping me happy should be a top priority for this program."

Many donors would find this attitude arrogant and unappealing.

Now consider the same donor and the same department head, but with you as the speaker:

> "Barbara is the best in her field."

> "She is a world-renowned scholar."

> "She is a great asset to our college."

> "Without her, this department wouldn't be anywhere near as strong as it is."

> "Retaining Barbara and keeping her happy is a top priority for me as the dean."

The same message has been conveyed, but coming from you, it invites the donor into a partnership with you in supporting Barbara. You can gracefully transition from your praise of Barbara into a solicitation: "I've invested significant college resources in Barbara and her department. I hope you'll join me in supporting her."

Now substitute yourself for the department head and the president for you. Touting your own greatness may not endear you to donors. The president's touting your greatness will confirm for donors that you are as terrific as they have come to believe. It will confirm that by supporting you and your program, they are investing in a high-profile, high-priority program at the university level.

As you have cultivated your relationship with a potential donor, you have learned what the donor's values and priorities are. If respect and affirmation are important to this donor, bringing a top campus leader into the relationship may be a necessity for a successful solicitation. Sometimes CEOs want to deal with CEOs. You are the CEO of your program, but a university CEO is above you. A donor's desire to engage with this top-level leader does not indicate that the donor does not respect you. It is merely a component of this donor's thought process and reflects a level at which he or she feels most comfortable making significant decisions. It may be a desire on the donor's part to be sure that your institution truly respects him or her. We often see this interest in alumni who have come a very long way in life from where they began as students. Being treated by the head of your institution as an equal can be a powerful validation of all the donor has accomplished. This can inspire in the donor feelings of gratitude for your program for having given him or her the tools to get started on the journey to success.

A top campus leader can help close a solicitation that has stalled. You and your development officer may have tried repeatedly to close the ask for a large gift. The donor seems receptive but will not commit. Introducing your president into the conversation at this point may provide a jump-start. The president can acknowledge that he or she is aware of the open ask and would like to be helpful to the donor in any way possible. This will likely evoke a more specific reply from the donor, whether positive or negative. If it does not and the donor still seems reluctant to commit, you probably have some more cultivation to do to get to a solicitation that will excite the donor enough to make a commitment.

Your Role with the President

Along with the benefits of a top leader's involvement with your donors, there can be risks as well. Before you ask your leader to step into your program, assess your institution's policies and practices about top-level engagement to ensure that you know what to expect. At some universities, the engagement of the president with a donor signals the end of your direct involvement, as well as your development officer's involvement. In these programs, top donor relationships are nurtured by one or two senior fundraisers working in close concert with the president. Sometimes the donors are encouraged to support the program that first identified and cultivated them, but often they are steered toward the president's own priorities. If the donor is passionately committed to your program, the gift may still come your way. But in the absence of your continued voice in the relationship, the donor may develop a stronger affinity for whatever program the president is emphasizing.

In environments like this, senior administrators and their development officers become reluctant to share information about their budding donor relationships. They fear that if the leadership of the campus development operation knows of a donor's potential, management of the relationship will be taken away and given to the president. This creates an atmosphere in which no one is able to provide the donor with the full breadth of opportunities to engage with the university. And in the long run, it undermines the university's likelihood of securing the largest possible gift from this donor.

A healthier and more effective program values all staff members' participation in developing donor relationships. The involvement of senior leadership from within the academy and from the development office will enhance rather than replace the relationships you and your program-based development staff have already established with the donor. A collaborative approach to developing a strategy for cultivation and solicitation will have a greater likelihood of success. The donor will observe that you are collegial and are working together to create a great program. This will help confirm the donor's confidence in you and your institution.

I recommend against withholding information or pitting your officer against the leadership of the development team. However, I do encourage caution if your university environment resembles the former of these examples. Before relinquishing your role with a donor to the president, be sure that you have done everything possible to engage the donor and inspire his or her loyalty to your program. Then if you must hand over the relationship, you can at least have hope that the donor's commitment to you and your program will guide his or her decisions, regardless of what other campus programs and priorities may be presented.

If you are in a collegial environment, be strategic about when you ask for senior leadership's involvement. The demands on your president's time are at least as heavy as your own, and probably more so. If you take him or her a development opportunity, be sure that it has a high likelihood of success and that it will be a good use of the leader's time. Your development officer carefully evaluates which donors truly need your engagement to make his or her best gift. Use the same process to evaluate whether a donor truly needs the leader's engagement to make his or her best gift.

Certainly every donor could enjoy meeting the president, but giving all of them this opportunity is unrealistic. Choose carefully a select few, and develop a strong case to present to your, and the development office's, senior leadership.

In presenting your request for leadership's time and involvement, emphasize:

- What you have done to initiate and cultivate the relationship

- The donor's financial potential

- Your assessment of the donor's readiness to make a large gift

- The areas in which the donor has expressed significant interest

- How this donor's support will tie to senior leadership's expressed priorities

- The strategy for the president or other senior leader's involvement in the relationship

Your goal is to persuade leadership that this will have a successful outcome. In a large university, and especially if you lead a small program in a large university, you may be competing with other colleges' and units' requests for your president's involvement. Your best likelihood of success is to show the top leader how this gift will mesh with his or her goals.

Once your leader has agreed to become involved, suggest a set of action steps to introduce the leader into the relationship with the donor. This gives you an opportunity to show your president your own proficiency in development and deepen your relationship with him or her. Take the lead in articulating who will play what role, especially when it is time to make the ask. Be sure to keep the president informed about any new developments that occur between his or her encounters with the donor. Remember to thank the president for his or her time. That is a donation in itself.

Your top institutional leadership will most often work with the university's top development staff. It is in your best interest to position your development officer to be engaged in the president's activities as well. This provides continuity for the donor. It also provides professional development for your officer and increases your likelihood of retaining a good staff member. It is demoralizing for a development officer to do the hard work of identifying and engaging a prospective donor, only to have the relationship taken over by other staff once the donor's high level of potential is identified. If your campus's senior development leadership does not recognize this, be assertive in advocating for your officer's continued involvement. This will send a strong, positive message to your officer, regardless of whether your request is granted.

Ideally your relationship with the donor will still be the primary one over the long term, even after your leadership has become involved. Do not lessen your ongoing engagement just because someone more senior than you has also connected with the donor. You and your development officer should continue to develop your strategies for the overall relationship with the donor because the president's relationship will probably focus almost exclusively on securing the gift.

20

Working with Donors Across Program Lines

Donors who are loyal to your program as graduates may also have interests in other programs on campus. They may have a passion around an issue that is not compartmentalized to just your program.

Interdisciplinary Projects

Universities play an important role in addressing complex problems and opportunities. Donors recognize that we bring multiple disciplines and perspectives to a project when faculty collaborate across departmental lines. This can create powerful outcomes that inspire donors to make large gifts.

However, at many universities, faculty members focus intently on their own work in their own departments. It is not uncommon for faculty from several disciplines to be working on various aspects of a single topic. These faculty may be acquainted with each other's work, but it is equally likely that they are not. Each of these programs will seek support from donors for their work. Some will be successful, and the support they garner will be focused as narrowly as the faculty's work is focused.

Consider an alternate approach. The faculty across the university working on a common topic come together. The provost and unit leaders combine the various faculty approaches into a multifaceted project that addresses the common issue on several fronts.

Now the president can approach these same donors from a completely different perspective. The president can ask for a leadership gift to address this problem in a sophisticated way. This shows the donor the university's commitment to addressing the issue and the expertise those working on it bring to the challenge. Attacking a problem in a coordinated way from multiple directions is more effective than chipping away at narrow components one at a time. This coordinated approach is likely to inspire donors to make investments that are far greater than the sum of the small gifts they might have given in response to the multiple appeals described earlier.

Fostering Collaboration

Fostering effective collaborations within the academy is a broad topic—too broad to address in depth in a book on fundraising. Here I limit the focus to some principles that will be important in securing high-end donor interest in collaborative projects.

There must be a clear statement of what the collaboration is intended to accomplish, and all members of the team must be committed to this understanding. Settle any disagreements or arguments before engaging with a prospective donor.

Donors will want to see someone as the spokesperson for the project. Having a point person reassures them that there is a combined strategy and that someone is responsible for keeping the project moving. This should also be the person who delivers regular progress reports to the donors from across the entire project team.

Communication with donors should be carefully coordinated and monitored so they hear consistent messages about the intention of the project, the plans, and the progress. Be sure that all the faculty who will have contact with the donor will do so in a constructive way.

Although there may be squabbles and turf battles within the collaboration, these must never come to the attention of donors.

Disagreements may sow seeds of doubt in their minds about whether this project is going to work.

Donors with Multiple Interests

Donors affiliate with institutions in many ways. Deans may work with couples in which one partner is a graduate of their college and the other is a graduate of another program within the university. Individuals may have degrees from multiple colleges within your university. Your graduates may also be interested in supporting areas that were important to them as students or are important to them now in the professional or civic realms.

Chapter Four addressed the principles of prospect management and the importance of treating donors with respect as we attempt to engage with them. Coordinated prospect management is especially important when donors are interested in more than one program on your campus. It is natural to be concerned that their interest in other areas may diminish their support for your program. Remember that they will make those decisions whether you are helpful to them in their broad relationship or not. You will benefit more by engaging with them across multiple interests than you will by clinging tightly to them or trying to discourage them from engaging with your campus colleagues.

When working with such donors, be sure you know who is coordinating the relationship (the prospect manager). The development officer plays an important role in communicating with the prospect manager and any other development staff who are working with these donors. You and your staff member should find out who is developing the solicitation plans and what the full range of campus involvement is.

As I noted in Chapter Four, some development programs operate on a philosophy of tight control over prospect management. There may be a centrally driven strategy for these donors that does not involve a direct role for you. It may be that a more enlightened view is gradually spreading throughout the development field, but your campus development office may not embrace it yet. If this is the case, take the initiative to have discussions among all the program leaders who have an interest in these donors, and include your development officers. Together, agree on the roles each of you would like to play.

As a group, approach the central development manager who enforces this approach. Share with this colleague your interest in working as a team in this donor relationship. You may need to include your provost or president in this conversation as well, especially if one of them has chosen to take the lead in the relationship. A group of academics offering constructive participation is hard to resist. By approaching this in a positive manner, you may be able to begin the transition of your development office's practices toward a more open approach to these complex donor relationships.

Clear, complete communication is a must in these situations. If you or other senior administrators try to circumvent the coordinated strategy by dealing with the donor outside the plan, you will likely put the donor in an awkward position. Donors do not want us to fight internally, and they especially do not want to be the cause of infighting.

Donors to Other Programs

I offer a caution about approaching individuals who are giving to other programs but not to yours.

A wealthy donor who has given a large gift to another area of your university looks appealing. You may hope that if you could get access to this wealthy patron, you too would receive a large gift. Most often, this would not be the case, however. The motivations that drove that large gift were particular to the area the donor supported. If the donor does not have a similar passion for your program, he or she will not give a similar gift regardless of how great your program is or how persuasive you are. Donors with major wealth tend to be strategic in their philanthropy and make their choices according to their own criteria. Merely getting access to them will not help you get a gift if your program is not perfectly aligned with their priorities.

If you do think there is such an alignment, reach out to the head of the program the donor supports to explore this possibility. Do not go directly to the donor because this will engender distrust and suspicion from your colleague, and the donor may sense that. Be prepared to make your case to your fellow academic, or the president or key relationship manager, as to why you think your program is a fit with the donor's interests. If your case is not well received, respect the decision. Do not pursue your strategy in a clandestine fashion.

If you find yourself on the other side of this situation—another unit head wants to approach a donor to your program—it is wise to be open to the possibility. If there does seem to be a connection, resist the urge to reject the possibility out of hand, and offer to approach the donor about the idea. You can share information about the other program and ask the donor if he or she would like to meet the other university representative. The more components of our university the donor values, the deeper the overall relationship will be. And the largest gifts come from the deepest relationships.

21

Engaging Your Own Community

Establishing a culture of philanthropy throughout your program begins with your own giving behavior. You should give to the annual fund every year and make occasional larger gifts as you are able. Donors will respect that you value your program as a philanthropic priority, not just as a job. By giving, you demonstrate to faculty and staff that you are serious about private support.

Engaging Faculty and Staff

The activities of your development program should be widely visible to your community, especially if you are building a program. Include your development officer in your cabinet meetings and faculty meetings as both an attendee and a presenter. A standing presentation on development at faculty meetings could include a report on progress toward annual goals and any special initiative or campaign goals, along with a story or two regarding new commitments. In particular, the reports should include a reference to everyone who participated in securing the gift.

Faculty who are unaware of the importance of academics to the development process may misinterpret your decreased engagement in routine administrative activities as your development work increases. Highlighting your activities in these development reports will help them understand how you are using your time when you are away.

These anecdotes also show faculty how they can become involved in working with donors. Some may become interested in increasing support for their program or gaining experience that will help them compete successfully as they advance their careers into higher-level administrative positions. Encourage them to contact the development staff to explore how they can contribute to the process.

Faculty often have information about graduates of their departments that is more extensive and current than that in the general alumni database. They can help the development staff by sharing this information and contacting their graduates to set up meetings. They can participate in donor visits as well. If they wish to learn how to ask for gifts themselves, they can join development officers on solicitation calls. Throughout their involvement, they should be diligent about communicating with the development staff. This will ensure that all efforts are coordinated and that donors do not receive mixed messages or overlapping approaches.

It is important to create in your community a realistic understanding of the role that fundraising can play in addressing your program's needs. Your limited development staff resources, along with the nature of your pool of potential supporters, may mean that you are not able to generate all the funds that all of your faculty would like to have. Communicating with your faculty, especially the department chairs, about how you are setting development goals and priorities gives them insight into how the development staff will be deploying themselves. Departments may ask the development staff to raise money for their programs. The development staff should never appear to be playing favorites by choosing which departments they will assist. An established list of priorities gives the staff a framework within which to respond to these requests.

Some of your administrative staff will also play a role in donor relationships. Consider donor encounters when they call or visit your program. Friendly, helpful staff make a good impression and convey a message of professionalism about your operation.

Students

Students play a vital role in your development programs. Involving them as guests at events and in campus visits with donors can create meaningful interactions for both. Learning firsthand about the interests and accomplishments of students deepens donors' engagement with your program by giving them a tangible representation of the importance of your work. Students gain perspective on the alumni community they have joined. They get direct access to observations and advice from those who have gone before them. Students who are preparing for competitive postgraduate scholarships and fellowships can incorporate encounters with donors into their process of polishing their professional presentation skills.

It is common to connect student scholarship recipients with the donors who funded their scholarships. A thank-you note from or an in-person visit by the student has a powerful effect on the donor. When students are informed of their scholarship awards, they should also receive information on how they are expected to thank the donor. The development office can facilitate this communication by providing sample language for notes and delivering the notes to the donor. If a face-to-face meeting is warranted, the development staff should set it up and attend. Direct, independent contact between students and donors, however, can go awry and should not be encouraged. For example, the student may misunderstand the parameters of the donor's support and ask the donor directly for additional funds.

Remember too that your students will one day be your donor prospects. While they are students, share with them the role that philanthropy plays in providing their education. An effective way to do this is to calculate the "hidden scholarship" that all students receive—that is, the difference between the tuition rate and the actual cost of delivering their education. Even a student whose family is paying full tuition is being subsidized in part by donors. Students who understand that they are being helped by donors will be well prepared to respond positively when they are solicited as alumni.

Soliciting Faculty and Staff

Internal fundraising campaigns offer your faculty and staff an opportunity to demonstrate their philanthropic support of your program, just as you yourself do with your own giving. Those who make gifts derive satisfaction and pride from their additional commitment to the work of your program. These campaigns can have a downside as well, particularly if budgets have been tight and salary increases minimal or nonexistent. Soliciting under these conditions may have a negative effect on morale that outweighs any benefits attained by the initiative. Rising faculty may also have concerns that their giving, or, more important, not giving, may play a role in their tenure process.

The best approach to a faculty or staff campaign, both to mitigate risks and to inspire participation, is to have the campaign initiated and led by peers. Your program's culture should determine whether there are separate approaches to faculty and staff or whether a single volunteer group with representation from both categories leads the effort. The peer volunteer leaders can share personal perspectives on why they give and can provide others with a rationale for doing so as well. Donors should have the option of giving anonymously, with no information about participation shared with their managers if they prefer.

Faculty can also be good prospects for major gifts and planned gifts. In particular, emeriti faculty with significant retirement funds can incorporate gifts into their estate plans. The development staff should provide current faculty with information on major and planned gift opportunities on a regular basis. The staff should maintain a reactive, rather than proactive, approach to these potential donor relationships, for the reasons identified earlier. Once faculty members have retired, the approach can become more assertive. Development officers can contact retired faculty members much as they would potential donors among the alumni constituency.

22

For Presidents and Provosts

Presidents and provosts have important development roles both on and off campus. Very large gifts, particularly those in the millions of dollars, rarely happen without the involvement of the most senior leadership of the university. And you set the example that deans and other senior administrators will follow. The amount of time you spend on development, and where it falls in your priorities, send a strong signal to academic leaders about where it should fit into theirs.

Your basic work with donors is similar to that of the deans and program heads, and you can use the same principles provided to them throughout this book. There are additional development considerations that are specific to your position.

Presidents

Most university presidents are expected to engage in fundraising. It is likely to be in your job description and in the criteria your board uses to evaluate your performance. You will have a portfolio of donor relationships and will work in partnership with the chief development officer of your campus to secure top-level gifts.

Your relationships with donors fall into three broad categories:

- Those where you are the primary contact, without whom the donor will not give

- Those where you are part of the relationship but someone else plays the primary role (usually an academic)

- Those where you engage briefly to provide endorsement of and support for a solicitation

Your chief development officer will identify opportunities for you among the many prospects and donors in your campus's overall portfolio. These will likely include board members and donors and prospects with the largest giving capacity. The number of relationships in which you should play the lead role is dependent on the portion of time you devote to development. Even the most engaged presidents can be the primary driver of only a relatively small portfolio of relationships—probably no more than two dozen. The vast demands on your time, along with the intense involvement inherent in being the primary driver, require that this number stay small for you to be effective.

These primary relationships should be with donors who have the capacity to transform programs or even the entire university. A successful university development program will have tens of thousands of donors. The few with whom you engage deeply should be at the narrow top of the overall donor pyramid.

Often these donors have developed an affinity for a component of the university before you enter the relationship. They may have established relationships with an academic leader, development officers, and other campus representatives. Some campuses have a policy that when a donor reaches a certain level of giving capacity, the relationship moves entirely into the domain of the president and the campus chief development officer. It is appropriate for the two of you to lead the strategy with the highest-level donors. But do not excise your colleagues from the relationship. The donor may feel loyal to the program head and want to maintain that contact, or may see the development officer as his or her main point of contact for logistical matters well beyond gifts. Keeping the full team engaged can provide the donor with a wider comfort zone. It also gives your academic administrators and development officers valuable experience in working with you and with a donor of this magnitude.

When you are brought into a relationship with a significant prospect, it is important to be well briefed on what the university already knows about the prospect's interests and goals. It can be tempting to promote your own priorities with these donors, to the exclusion of other projects their academic contact may have presented. But this puts donors in the awkward position of having to choose whether to favor the head of their program or the president. It also creates an environment where academic leaders are hesitant to inform you, or your development vice president, about significant prospects for fear that the prospects will be pressured to give to another area. If you follow the principles covered in this book and make the donor's interests the top priority, you may find that the donor will expand his or her philanthropic interest and give to both areas.

Some donors may not be interested in working with you on their gifts. If your development officer shares that information with you, accept the donor's wishes. It is unlikely that this is a personal reflection on you. More commonly, it is an indication of the donor's deeply connected relationship with another campus representative. If that is where the donor is most comfortable, the university will see better, larger gifts by respecting the donor's preference.

Relationships where you are a secondary member of the team will take less of your time. Generally these are donors whose gifts are at a level of significance within the campus's overall donor constituency, but whose affiliation with the unit they support is so deep that the primary relationship is with that unit head. In these cases, you convey the gratitude and respect of the campus for both the donor's generosity and the importance of the program he or she supports. It is not uncommon for your primary role in these relationships to be one of stewardship rather than solicitation.

In the final category, where you engage only briefly, your role is generally to provide an endorsement of the solicitation. Chapter Nineteen covered how academic leaders can involve you in this capacity. In some cases, the donor needs to know that the project or program has the president's blessing. These gifts may not be at the level where you would normally become involved. However, the minimal time required for you to have one or two meetings and provide your endorsement may make the difference between a small gift and a significant one.

Provosts

Most provosts do not play a significant external role in development, but your internal role is invaluable. As you hire, manage, and evaluate deans, you establish expectations for their development performance. Even if you are not directly involved in donor work, you must understand development sufficiently to be able to articulate expectations and assess performance.

Your relationship with the campus's chief development officer is critical. The two of you must be able to discuss the academics' development performance with complete candor and trust. The vice president, or a senior manager on his or her staff, should meet deanship candidates as a standard part of the interview process and give you his or her assessment of the candidates' fundraising potential. You and the vice president should also confer on the deployment of development resources throughout the campus. Decisions about centralizing or decentralizing development activities should be made jointly because you both will live with the consequences of the choices you make.

The chief development officer can help you determine the specific evaluation criteria you will use in assessing your deans' development work. Incorporating development metrics into your regular management and budget discussions with deans is a good technique for reinforcing the fundamental nature of this work within their portfolio of responsibilities.

Deans will not always be in complete agreement with the development office, and you may find yourself in the role of adjudicator. A well-established relationship with the vice president, along with a clear understanding of the campus's fund-raising approaches and objectives, will serve you well in these situations.

When multiple units are involved in a donor relationship, you may need to serve as convener of the project leadership. Development officers can create a strategy for engaging the donor, but we should not make decisions about how each college or program participates in the project and its funding. Your development colleagues rely on you to ensure that the collaboration is consistent with overall priorities and is being implemented in an appropriate fashion programmatically.

If you are a provost who would like to work directly with donors, tell your development vice president. Ask for help in identifying appropriate opportunities. You may be able to play a role in support of your deans similar to that described for presidents. You may be the ideal primary contact in donor relationships that span multiple colleges.

23

Leadership Transitions

Changes in leadership inevitably result in a period of destabilization in a program, even when the transition is a positive one. If you are a party in the transition, you can help the development program maintain forward momentum during this period. If the transition is occurring above you, you may have to adjust your development efforts to accommodate both the departure and the arrival of new leadership.

Your Predecessor

The relationships that donors develop with their campus partners should be focused on the university, not on the individual representative of the university. But even with this professional approach, such partnerships may also become personal friendships over time. When the university contact moves on, the professional component of these relationships can be transferred to the departed leader's replacement. Donors naturally expect the new leader to take charge of the program. The transition of the personal component of the partnership may be less straightforward, however.

As a new program head, you may hear positive commentary about your predecessor from donors, particularly if he or she was a long-sitting, successful leader. You may be encountering problems left behind by your predecessor, and you may have been brought into the position to effect change from the prior leader's approach.

Donors who supported your program during the prior leader's time in office may not know much, if anything at all, about any internal issues, nor should they. It can be difficult to hear your predecessor deified by donors as you are dealing with the difficulties he or she left behind.

Your interactions with donors about the prior leader should remain professional and positive. Any attempt to share your predecessor's shortcomings is likely to create a breach between you and the donors. They will be uncomfortable to hear negative information about an administrator they chose to support, and they are likely to distance themselves from you as a result. Accept the fond reminiscences without encouraging them. Over time the donors' focus on your predecessor will subside, and they will create their own positive relationships with you.

Once you have established the directions in which you plan to take your program, share this information with donors. Do not present these plans as addressing areas that are substandard and need to be fixed, because donors will infer a criticism of the prior leader in that approach. This is particularly important in areas that have had strong donor support. If you criticize prior directions in that area, you are by extension conveying that their support was misguided or misused. Rather, share your intentions as plans to take your program even further in its growth.

Your most challenging group may be a preexisting leadership volunteer group. Your development officer may be able to give you insight into this group's relationship with your predecessor. If the majority of the members were recruited by the prior administrator based on strong relationships with that person, you may find resistance from that group as you begin to implement changes in the program. Some members may feel disloyal to the prior leader if they support a different direction. Give the group time to get to know you and to learn about your priorities and plans. They may come to support you as enthusiastically as they supported your predecessor. If there are members who do not seem to be able to transfer their allegiance, eventually you may have to replace them.

If any of your predecessors are still present in your program community, consider whether they can be an asset to your development efforts. This is primarily effective with prior administrators who have retired in good standing. They should absent themselves from view until you are well established. At that point, if they are still nearby or on the faculty, confer with your development staff about whether there is a role for emeriti academics in your efforts. A good example of this is having an emeritus academic serve as honorary chair of a fundraising campaign or initiative. This person's endorsement encourages donors to support you, and may be important for some loyalists who otherwise might not wish to accept you.

Maintaining Momentum During a Presidential Transition

You and your development officer can assess the relationships a departing president has had with donors to your program. While the news of the departure should go to those donors from the president or through other official channels, you should communicate with them as soon as it becomes appropriate to do so.

If you are considering launching a major initiative, it may be best to delay the launch until the leadership transition has concluded. It can be difficult to advance new projects during a lame duck presidency, an interim presidency, and the early days of a new presidency. And if your project is not consistent with the priorities of the new president, the project itself may become a lame duck.

Once the new president is named, be assertive in briefing him or her about your development plans and initiatives and asking for help in targeted ways. Include the vice president for development in this process. As the vice president helps the new president establish a donor portfolio, the requests you have made will be top of mind for both of them.

You can use the techniques discussed in Chapter Nineteen to catch the attention of your new leader. In some cases, you may need to alter your messages to ensure that they are consistent with the new president's messages. It is not necessary to change your priorities. Rather, review the way you are presenting them to ensure that you are in sync with the new president's announced preferences.

Look for ways to engage the new president with your donors. This positions you as a helpful colleague to the new president and shows your constituency that the president places value on your program.

Weathering the Departure of a High-Profile Faculty Member

Losing a faculty member who has strong donor relationships puts you at significant risk of losing those gifts as well. If the faculty member is leaving for another institution, donors may follow the faculty member to the new university. Discuss with your development officer and the faculty member, if the departure is amicable, who should receive the news in advance of a public announcement. You should make these calls yourself and be prepared to share with the donors how you are planning to adapt to the faculty member's absence.

If the faculty member is retiring, donors may continue their support. The point of retirement is a natural time to implement a focused effort to raise funds for a gift in honor of the faculty member's career. These honorary gift funds tend to be small, no matter how beloved the professor may have been. An endowed scholarship is a good baseline target. Do not aim for a high-level fund unless a donor has emerged to contribute a very large gift. Otherwise you may embarrass the retiring faculty member by being unable to garner enough support to fund the honor.

In the wake of a high-profile departure, you may decide to make significant changes to that area of your program. Be candid with donors about what you are doing and why you have chosen this path. You do not have to tell them everything, but once you have made decisions, meet with any high-level donor to share what you are doing. You may lose some of them over these changes, but others will welcome the new direction and join you in supporting it.

Preparing for Your Own Departure

When you decide to leave, one of the first people you should tell is your development officer. He or she will need time to prepare a communications plan for sharing the news with donors. Some of these donors need to hear the news before it is publicly announced, preferably from you personally.

If you are retiring, ask your development officer to recommend a series of development activities for you to complete before you step down. Some of these may involve travel to see individual donors or attend group events. As this process moves along, you may find that the frequent repetition of the reason for your decision and your plans for the future wears on you. Remember that for each donor, this is new information. Their interest is an indication of the level of esteem in which they hold you and your program. Giving them the opportunity to express their individual reactions to your departure is a way for you to support them as they have supported you.

The same cautions about honorary gifts for retiring faculty apply here as well. Your development officer can ascertain whether there is interest among the donor constituency in establishing a fund in your honor. If there is, choose a designation that is consistent with your priorities as the program head. Do not be discouraged if the initiative does not raise a large sum of money. The fund may grow over time, and you can contribute to it yourself during your emeritus years.

When moving to another position, the time frame of your departure is likely to be much shorter than with a retirement. Although you should confer with your development officer regarding donors who should receive advance notice, you will have fewer farewell meetings. In many cases your program's top donors will meet with your manager, not with you, as the university seeks to reassure donors regarding continuity of the program on your departure.

Do not attempt to lure donors with you to the new program. Donors give to causes that align with their passions. If their passions are with you personally, they will follow you of their own accord. If their passions are with your program and university, attempting to sway their interests will not work, and it will likely tarnish your reputation with university leadership.

Whatever the circumstances of your departure, do not expect to maintain the same level of friendship with individual donors that you have enjoyed in your previous position. In some cases, the personal component of the relationship may carry on. But that is the exception, not the rule. Most donors, even those with whom you have the closest relationships, will focus on getting to know the new leader and may keep in touch with you only peripherally. In all cases, let donors set the tone of the new relationship.

Case Study

Coordinating Donor Relationships Across Programs

Donna Donor and Sam Supporter are both graduates of Sample University. Donna graduated from the College of Pharmacy and has become a successful executive in the medical devices industry. Sam Supporter graduated from the College of Journalism. He is a high-profile sports reporter for a major television network. Donna and Sam were college sweethearts who married in their late twenties. They have lived in the university's area since graduation. Over the past thirty-five years as alumni, they have stayed involved with the campus.

Sam is heavily involved in the football booster club. He contributes to the athletics fund every year and has served in a number of leadership positions within the club. He has also been a regular volunteer for the College of Journalism. He has spoken to classes and student clubs and has arranged for student groups to take tours at his network offices.

Donna has maintained close relationships with several faculty members. They have interacted within professional organizations in the pharmaceutical industry, and Donna's company has research contracts with several programs and faculty in the College of Pharmacy. She has also established an internship program at her company for pharmacy students.

Donna and Sam's relationships with their programs evolved somewhat independently for the first three decades after college. They responded to annual fund mailings from each of their colleges and from the athletics program, gradually increasing their annual gifts over the years. They attained membership in the programs' giving societies by donating more than $1,000 to each of their three areas of interest every year. From time to time, they made a larger gift to mark a special occasion or project. For example, they gave $10,000 in honor of Sam's thesis adviser when he retired from the faculty.

As they entered their early fifties, with their children grown and on their own, Sam and Donna became even more involved with the university. Donna was invited to serve on the search committee for a new dean in pharmacy. Sam became the president of the football booster club and was a vocal fan of the coaches and their results.

The development officers from journalism, pharmacy, and athletics had long kept each other informed of their activities with the couple. When Donna and Sam were scheduled to sit in the president's box at a football game, the athletics development officer alerted the other two officers. They then had their deans stop by the box to chat with Donna and Sam during the game. When Sam was going to be on campus to lecture in journalism, that development officer would alert the athletics development officer, who would issue an invitation for Sam to stop by the athletics complex for coffee before or after the lecture.

Pharmacy was preparing for a major initiative to raise funds for graduate student fellowships, and was hoping Donna would make a major gift to the project. The pharmacy development officer mentioned this to her colleagues in journalism and athletics. She learned that athletics was thinking the time was right to solicit Sam for a gift to establish an endowed scholarship for a football player. And journalism had similar plans for a large ask to support an internship program.

The three development officers recognized the importance of coordinating these asks so that Sam and Donna did not perceive the programs to be competing for their philanthropic support.

They also recognized that the two deans and the athletic director would each want to be the first to ask for a major gift. They recommended a group strategy session to determine how to proceed.

The vice president for development facilitated the session, which all three unit heads and all three development officers attended. Each program's representatives explained their rationale for wanting to approach Sam, Donna, or both for a significant commitment. They described the projects they believed the couple would like to support. It was clear that the three units had two major perceptions in common.

First, they all agreed that Sam and Donna were well positioned for a successful solicitation. Each unit had cultivated an individual relationship with Sam or Donna. They knew the deans and the athletic director and had positive feelings about all three. They had shown steadily increasing giving behavior and had always responded favorably to targeted solicitations. They were both successful in their careers and appeared to be comfortable financially.

Second, they all agreed that Donna and Sam's main priority at the university was students. Most of their engagement activities had involved students, and they clearly enjoyed their opportunities to interact with students.

Each of the unit heads was ready to proceed with a solicitation for a major gift and eager to do so in the near future. Each was also concerned that soliciting Sam and Donna one at a time might result in a favorable response to the first solicitation, at the expense of the other two asks. The group discussed the possibility of requesting a meeting with the couple where all three unit heads would attend and would present their requests in a package.

While they liked the possibility of each unit's having a voice in the presentation, the group agreed that the meeting could become cumbersome. One of the deans was not comfortable actually asking for the gift and preferred having a development officer present to assist with that component of the conversation. That took attendance from the university to at least four people, and possibly more, because the other dean and the athletic director then wanted their development officers present as well.

The vice president proposed an alternate strategy. Donna and Sam had a close and friendly relationship with the president of the university. The vice president proposed that he and the president invite the couple to dinner and solicit an overall gift that would include components for each of the programs. The deans and the athletic director agreed, as long as they had an opportunity in advance of the meeting to make their case to the president for their particular project.

The president was happy to play a role in the solicitation, as she enjoyed her relationship with the couple. She listened to the rationale from the unit heads for their respective projects. Pharmacy wanted to ask for $150,000. Athletics had intended to ask for $100,000, and journalism had intended to ask for $50,000, but both units raised their request to $150,000 after hearing that pharmacy had targeted the higher amount. The president and vice president decided to ask Sam and Donna for a $500,000 gift, to be divided essentially equally among the three programs.

The invitation to Sam and Donna was issued by the vice president. He e-mailed them both, saying that he and the president would like to have dinner with them to explore some opportunities for deepening their generous support of the university. They agreed, and their assistants identified a date three weeks later for the dinner to take place.

The president suggested a restaurant several neighborhoods away from the university. She wanted to be sure they could have their conversation with some assurance of privacy. The dinner began with casual conversation about families and current events. The long-standing relationships the president and vice president had with Sam and Donna allowed this early conversation to be relaxed and to meander through a variety of subjects without focusing particularly on the university.

Once the entrées had arrived, the president raised the business of the evening. She referenced the vice president's e-mail and said that she appreciated Donna and Sam's giving them an opportunity to present some ideas for their consideration. She began by focusing on students:

> We deeply appreciate the opportunities you've provided our students over the years. You've enriched their educational experiences, and we're very grateful to you.

She then acknowledged their involvement with the three programs:

> I know the deans and the athletic director appreciate all you do for them. We're fortunate to have such a committed alumni couple in our university family.

She moved on to provide her endorsement of the programs:

> We have terrific leadership in all three of these programs. It was such a coup to recruit the new dean in pharmacy, and we couldn't be happier with the dean of journalism and with our football coaches.

Then she offered the umbrella ask:

> We wanted to get together with you tonight to ask if you would consider making a major financial commitment to the university, one that would benefit students in all three of the areas you support.

Donna and Sam agreed that they would consider this. It was clear to the president and the vice president that the couple had been expecting the solicitation. Given the positive reaction, the vice president moved into the specific solicitation. He gave a brief overview of the three projects to set the stage. Then he asked for the specific amount:

> A gift of $500,000 to endow the Donna Donor and Sam Supporter Fund for Student Excellence would enable us to move forward with all three of these projects.

He went on to delineate how many students would be affected in each program if the fund were endowed at that level.

As the conversation progressed, Sam and Donna expressed a positive reaction to the overall idea. They asked questions about how quickly the internship program could be established and when the scholarships and fellowships could be awarded. They gave no feedback about the dollar amount of the ask.

The conversation ended with Sam suggesting that he and Donna would talk about the request and get back to the president with their reaction within the next couple of weeks. The rest of the dinner proceeded with friendly conversation. As the group parted in the parking lot, the president returned to the solicitation conversation. She said:

> Thank you for giving us the opportunity to present our request. I am personally grateful for all the ways you have been generous to the university over the years, and I look forward to continuing our friendship long into the future.

The vice president shifted the next step away from the couple and back to the university by saying:

> Yes, thank you for your consideration. I have some materials from the programs with more detail about

each of their projects. How about if I send those to you tomorrow?

The vice president sent the materials and called two days later to ensure that they had arrived. He asked Donna, who had taken the call, if she and Sam had any questions or needed any further information. She assured him that they had everything they needed and were in the process of deciding what they would like to do.

The morning after the dinner, the president e-mailed Donna and Sam:

> It was great to see you last night. I want to reiterate how much we appreciate your long-standing support. You're the best!

A week after the dinner, Sam replied to that e-mail: "You're pretty great yourself! Our relationship with the university means everything to us, and we want to do whatever we can for the students. We've thought about your request and have decided to establish the fund you proposed with $300,000 before year's end. We'll then increase it with $100,000 gifts in each of the next two years to get it fully funded. We'd like to be able to do it all right now, but our cash position doesn't allow that. We don't want to wait until it's all available, so we hope you'll be all right with starting smaller and growing."

The president called Sam and Donna's home phone number immediately upon receiving the e-mail. She left an effusive and excited message of thanks. She then replied to their e-mail with a similar message.

The vice president followed up with Sam and Donna to document their agreement, establish the fund, and assist with the transfer of stock for the initial $300,000. The deans and the athletic director sent their thanks as well.

Although Donna and Sam declined having a formal announcement of their gift, they agreed to an article in the alumni magazine the following year. The article profiled the newly named fellowship and scholarship recipients and described the internship program. In their interview for the article, Sam and Donna expressed their warm feelings about having established their fund: "Every student we meet is incredible. For us to be able to help them in some small way is enormously gratifying, and we are thrilled to have the opportunity to be a part of their lives."

Recommended Resources

Burk, P. *Donor-Centered Fundraising*. Hamilton, Ont.: Cygnus Applied Research, 2003.

Dove, K. E. *Conducting a Successful Capital Campaign*. San Francisco: Jossey-Bass, 2000.

Dove, K., Lindauer, J., and Madvic, C. *Conducting a Successful Annual Giving Program*. San Francisco: Jossey-Bass, 2001.

Hilenski, F. A. *Unit Development Officer's Handbook*. Washington, D.C.: CASE, 2002.

Kihlstedt, A. *Capital Campaigns: Strategies That Work*. Burlington, Mass.: Jones and Bartlett, 2010.

Lindahl, W. E. *Principles of Fundraising: Theory and Practice*. Burlington, Mass.: Jones and Bartlett, 2010.

McKinnon, H. *Eleven Questions Every Donor Asks and the Answers All Donors Crave: How You Can Inspire Someone to Give Generously*. Medfield, Mass.: Emerson and Church, 2008.

Prince, R. A., and File, K. M. *Seven Faces of Philanthropy*. San Francisco: Jossey-Bass, 2001.

Walker, J. I. *Nonprofit Essentials: Major Gifts*. Hoboken, N.J.: Wiley, 2006.

Acknowledgments

I thank the thousands of academics and development officers who have attended my training sessions over the past decade. Every time I teach, I learn from you.

My interest in working with academics was sparked by the late Lawrence B. Dumas, an extraordinary provost and an equally extraordinary man.

The Council for Advancement and Support of Education (CASE) has provided me with many edifying volunteer opportunities throughout my career. I am grateful to the dedicated CASE staff for their deep commitment to our profession and their support of my work.

The development team at the University of Illinois at Chicago is the finest group of professionals I have ever encountered. It is an honor to belong to and lead that team. I salute each of my colleagues for the fine work you do. I particularly thank Ray Vas for his partnership. I paid my dues for twenty years to earn the privilege of working with you every day.

Eric Gislason, Clark Hulse, Wesley Lindahl, and Sylvia Manning provided me with invaluable support during the process of writing this book. They gave me wise and helpful advice on writing and publishing. Their certainty that there was a need for this book, and that I should be the one to write it, gave me the courage to take this on.

The Creative Leap Club, under the leadership of Cynthia Morris, was the incubator for this project. Thank you to Mimi,

Mavis, Dora, Eileen, and Barbara for the environment of supportive accountability that kept me moving forward.

Anyone who is not convinced of the transformative power of executive coaching has not met Mary Jo Hazard, Master Certified Coach. Your coaching over the past decade has shown me that everything is possible.

Lisa Swanson, Chris Kennelly, and Charles Katzenmeyer took every step on the path of this book with me. Thank you for never once doubting that I could do it.

I am blessed with the best family I could ever hope to have. Bernie Hunt and Debbie Turner, I would love you even if I weren't related to you.

Above all, every day of my life is made better and brighter by the most interesting, creative, brilliant, funny, remarkable person I have ever met. Thank you for choosing me as your mom, Jaye.

The Author

Penelepe C. Hunt is a fundraiser, teacher, coach, and consultant with nearly thirty years of experience in higher education development.

As a fundraiser, Penny has a track record of building sustainable programs and directing transformational campaigns. She led the $1.5 billion Campaign Northwestern, which at the time was only the twelfth billion dollar fundraising effort in higher education.

As vice chancellor for development at the University of Illinois at Chicago (UIC), she built a development program that doubled its results in five years. Her team exceeded the $650 million campaign goal and secured the first eight-figure gifts in UIC's history. She created training programs for academics at UIC that include orientation for new deans, workshops for advanced deans, program head training, and a one-on-one faculty training program.

She has trained and coached thousands of academic leaders and development officers around the world. Her workshops and coaching sessions provide academics with practical guidance for finding, enjoying, and succeeding in their role in the development process. As a frequent presenter for the Council for Advancement and Support of Education (CASE), Penny has won the prestigious Steuben Apple Award for teaching excellence.

Index